Pain and Pleasure

Precious Joseph

Table of Contents

Chapter 1:
When I was a baby...

I was born in New Orleans, Louisiana, to Sylvia Joseph. My real father was absent, leaving my mother to fulfill both parental roles. My entry into the world was marred by complications. When my mother went into labor, her water broke prematurely, exposing me to harmful bacteria. Despite the odds, I survived, but not without consequences. I spent two to three precarious months in the hospital, fighting for my life.

During this time, my family rallied around me, reading, talking, and praying for my recovery. Despite the doctor's grim prognosis, my grandmother's unwavering faith sustained her belief that I would survive. Against all expectations, I eventually left the hospital, but the ordeal had lasting effects on my mother's health and my own.

As I grew older, the challenges persisted. Despite my determination, navigating the education system as a special education student was fraught with obstacles. Teachers questioned my placement in their classes, and family members exerted control over crucial decisions, especially regarding my education.

One of the most pivotal moments during my schooling came when I was on the brink of graduating high school. Despite my hard work and determination, the school administration hesitated to award me a diploma, opting for a certificate that marked me as different from my peers.

This decision weighed heavily on my mother, but my grandmother stepped in with unwavering resolve. She had always been my fiercest advocate, and she wasn't about to let me be treated differently just because of my learning challenges.

With determination in her eyes, she marched into the school, demanding to speak with the principal. She argued passionately for my right to be treated like any other student, insisting that I had worked just as hard and deserved the same recognition.

Her words carried weight, not just because of her fierce spirit, but because she spoke from a place of love and belief in my potential.

While my grandmother fought tirelessly for my right to be treated equally in school, another family member, my Aunt Ursula, held a different view. Ursula, for reasons known only to her, was adamant that I remain in special education classes, despite my capabilities.

Her influence cast a shadow over my educational journey, with teachers and administrators often deferring to her judgment instead of recognizing my potential. Ursula's insistence on keeping me in special education not only affected my academic progress but also took a toll on my self-esteem.

I remember the frustration and helplessness I felt as I watched my peers move forward while I remained stuck in classes that didn't challenge me. It was a constant reminder of the barriers I faced, not just in the classroom, but in life.

And from a young age, I bore the burden of what my family called "dark marks." They were birthmarks scattered across my face, a visible reminder of genetics beyond my control. To my family, they weren't just innocent pigmentation; they were a source of shame and scrutiny.

I still remember the whispers and stares whenever we visited relatives. Their eyes would inevitably drift to my face, their words tinged with pity or disdain. It wasn't just the strangers' reactions that hurt; it was the treatment I received from those closest to me.

My mother, though loving in her way, couldn't escape the influence of her upbringing. She, too, saw my birthmarks as something to be hidden or erased. I endured endless remedies and treatments in a desperate attempt to "fix" what was deemed unacceptable.

But perhaps the harshest treatment came from my aunt Ursula. She made no effort to conceal her disdain, often making cutting remarks about my appearance in front of others. It was as if my birthmarks were a reflection of some inherent flaw, a mark of inferiority that tainted everything I did.

As I grew older, the impact of their words and actions became harder to bear. I longed to be seen for who I was beyond the surface, but it seemed that my birthmarks would forever define me in the eyes of my family.

In addition to the verbal and emotional torment, my family's obsession with my birthmarks manifested in more insidious ways. They believed that by scrubbing my face relentlessly and depriving me of sweets, they could somehow erase the marks that marred my appearance.

I can still recall the sting of their words as they rationed out chocolates and candies, citing my "indulgence" as the cause of my blemishes. It was as if my very existence was a reminder of their discomfort, a flaw to be concealed and controlled at any cost.

But perhaps the most painful aspect of their treatment was their insistence on hiding my birthmarks from the world. They forbade me from wearing my hair in a ponytail, instead instructing me to let it fall in front of my face like a veil. It was a constant reminder that my appearance was something to be ashamed of, something to be hidden away from prying eyes.

I felt like a monster, condemned to live in the shadows of my skin. Every glance in the mirror was a confrontation with the ugliness they saw reflected at me. And as much as I longed to rebel against their restrictions, I couldn't shake the feeling of shame that had been ingrained in me from a young age.

It wasn't until my mother's revelation to the dermatologist that the truth began to emerge. My father, it turned out, had also borne the same birthmarks that plagued me. Suddenly, the shame and secrecy that had shrouded my existence began to lift.

I began carrying a deep curiosity about my father, a longing that seemed to grow with each passing year. I would pester my mother incessantly, begging for any scrap of information about him. But she would always deflect, brushing off my questions with a vague dismissal.

It wasn't until one day, perhaps sensing the weight of my curiosity, that she finally relented. 'Your dad's name is Sparrow Dillard,' she told me, her voice tinged with reluctance. It was a name that would echo in my mind for years to come, a tether to a man I had never known.

My older sister, who shared a different father, seemed unfazed by my relentless inquiries. But for me, the absence of a father figure felt like a void, a missing piece of the puzzle that made up my identity.

As I grew older, my mother revealed more about my father, painting a picture of a man with dark marks covering his face. It was a revelation that struck a chord within me as if I had finally found a piece of myself in his likeness.

But despite this newfound connection, the absence of my father left me feeling adrift, like a ship without a compass. I yearned for his presence, for the guidance and love that only a father could provide.

Though my mother did her best to fill the void, her love and care could never fully replace the missing piece of my heart. I felt like a puzzle with a piece missing, forever incomplete.

Looking back at my childhood photos, I saw a reflection of the sadness that had always lingered within me. Despite the smiles plastered on my face, there was a heaviness in my eyes, a weight that seemed too heavy for a child to bear.

Reflecting on my early struggles brings a mix of emotions, but it also serves as a testament to my resilience and the support of those who believed in me.

Though the hospital where my journey began may have closed its doors long ago, the memories and lessons from that time continue to shape who I am today.

One such memory and part of my childhood that shaped me was my speech impediment. It became a defining feature of my childhood, shaping the way I saw myself and how others perceived me. I struggled to articulate simple words, often leaving teachers perplexed and classmates amused. Even pronouncing my name was a challenge, with the letter 'P' proving particularly elusive. It was a constant source of frustration and embarrassment, reinforcing the belief that I was somehow deficient or flawed.

At home, the teasing from my cousins only compounded my insecurities. Their playful taunts cut deeper than they realized, leaving me feeling isolated and misunderstood. It was a stark reminder that even in the safety of my own family, I was different, an outsider looking in.

When I was held back in the first grade because of my speech issues, it felt like a betrayal of everything I had worked for. Despite excelling academically, I was judged solely on my ability to communicate. My mother's vague explanation only added to my confusion and disappointment, leaving me to grapple with feelings of inadequacy.

Watching my peers move on to the next grade while I remained behind was a bitter pill to swallow. I felt like I was being left behind, relegated to the sidelines while life passed me by. It took me some time to come to terms with the situation and to accept that my path might be different from others.

My mother was my unwavering pillar of support. Every Friday, without fail, she would take me to speech therapy classes, despite my reluctance. I resented those sessions, feeling like I was missing out on the fun my cousins were having at home. To me, it seemed like a futile endeavor, with the exercises feeling more like a chore than a path to improvement.

It wasn't until later that my mother revealed the true reason behind the therapy sessions - to secure a government check for my SSI disability. Despite the ulterior motive, her commitment to my well-being was unwavering, and I couldn't help but feel grateful for her efforts.

Other family members also played a significant role in supporting me through my challenges. Despite the stigma associated with learning disabilities, they rallied around me, offering encouragement and reassurance. Even when I wanted to give up, they urged me to persevere, reminding me that progress takes time and effort.

I particularly remember my Auntie Ursa's dedication to helping me succeed in her crooked sense of the word. In the third grade, she would sit with me in class, patiently guiding me through my assignments. Her presence embarrassed me, but despite the setbacks and the emotional toll it took on me, I harbored no resentment towards those who doubted or mistreated me. Forgiveness became my armor, allowing me to move forward despite the scars of my past.

My grandmother's love and encouragement were particularly impactful. Whenever I stumbled over words, she would patiently urge me to try again, instilling in me a sense of determination and resilience. Her unwavering belief in my abilities gave me the strength to keep pushing forward, even when the road seemed long and arduous.

One of the most cherished memories I hold from my childhood is the bond I shared with my uncle. Amidst the tumultuous currents of my upbringing, he stood as a steady beacon of warmth and understanding.

I recall countless occasions when I found myself lost in the labyrinth of my thoughts, feeling adrift in a sea of uncertainty. Sensing my distress, my uncle would approach with a gentle smile, his eyes brimming with compassion.

'Come inside,' he would say, his voice a soothing melody amidst the cacophony of my inner turmoil. 'Let's talk.'

Entering his kitchen, I would watch in awe as he moved with practiced ease, effortlessly transforming simple ingredients into culinary delights. The rhythmic clatter of pots and pans provided a comforting backdrop to our conversations, a symphony of familiarity that eased the tension in my heart.

As he stirred and seasoned, my uncle would listen attentively to my ramblings, offering sage advice and words of wisdom that resonated deep within my soul. His presence was a balm for my wounded spirit, his unconditional love a lifeline in times of need.

Together, we would sit at the kitchen table, savoring the meal he had prepared with such care. With each bite, the weight of my burdens would lift, replaced by a sense of peace and contentment that only his company could provide.

In those moments, surrounded by the warmth of his love and the aroma of home-cooked food, I felt truly seen and understood. My uncle's simple gesture of making something to eat while we talked was more than just a meal – it was a testament to the power of love to nourish both body and soul.

Chapter 2: Pockmarked Like Dad

When I think back to my childhood, I remember a time filled with physical and emotional challenges. At around 8 or 9 years old, I started noticing bumps on my face. This was just the beginning of a journey that would leave dark spots and shape my identity.

At first, my family didn't notice the bumps on my skin. They thought it was a normal part of growing up. But these marks didn't go away and started to cause me physical discomfort and emotional distress. I felt like everyone was staring at me and judging me because of these dark marks. It made me question my reflection and feel self-conscious.

My attempts to remedy the situation by picking at the bumps only exacerbated the issue, as the marks began to multiply and deepen. The transformation was swift, and I woke up one morning to face a person I hardly recognized—a face marred by dark spots that seemed to define me in the eyes of the world.

The ordeal became more daunting when I experienced the disdainful gaze of a peer, a girl who looked at me with a mixture of evil and hatred. The weight of walking around with these visible marks, coupled with the judgmental stares, became a daily struggle.

My family's initial attempts to find a solution focused on external factors—blaming my diet, restricting sweets, and trying various skincare products. The proactive commercials on TV became a recurring reminder of the ongoing battle with my appearance. My mother, in her attempts to reassure me, perpetually emphasized the cleanliness of my face whenever the topic arose.

Amidst the external efforts to address my condition, the emotional toll intensified. My auntie, Ursula, played a significant role in my daily routine, often administering treatments to my face. This ritual, however well-intentioned, heightened my sense of shame and self-consciousness.

As the marks extended beyond my face to my back and shoulders, the burden became even more burdensome. The constant documentation through pictures at dermatologist appointments added another layer to the struggle—I couldn't even see my skin beneath the layers of dark marks. The routine of applying multiple creams and following specific skincare rituals became a constant reminder of my perceived imperfections.

The shame and frustration reached a peak when my auntie Ursula, with genuine concern, would help me through the morning and night routines. The daily regimen, the endless scrutiny of my face, and the continuous discussions about my appearance became overwhelming.

The impact extended beyond the physical realm; it penetrated deep into my emotional well-being. The relentless focus on my skin overshadowed my sense of self, leaving me with a profound sense of inadequacy. The emotional scars, intertwined with the physical ones, became integral to my formative years.

During this struggle, the question of identity loomed large. Who was I beyond the dark marks that seemed to define me in the eyes of my family and society? The journey to answer this question would take unexpected turns, but the roots of resilience and strength planted during these challenging times would shape the person I was becoming.

Yet, amidst the struggle, there was a glimmer of hope—a realization that my worth extended beyond the surface, beyond the visible marks that told a limited story. Little did I know that this phase would be a stepping stone to a deeper understanding of self-acceptance and the unwavering support of those who saw beyond the marks to the person within.

As I navigated the complexities of my adolescence, the constant battle with my appearance remained a poignant theme in my life. My auntie Ursula, in her efforts to help me combat the dark marks, often visited to introduce new products and guide me through skincare routines. It became a routine—one that held the promise of a solution, yet also deepened my discomfort.

Despite the evolving skincare rituals, I developed a habit of avoiding my reflection. The mirror became a source of discomfort, a reminder of the person I didn't want to confront. My auntie's insistence on facing my reflection head-on forced me to confront the reality of my appearance, a reality I sought to escape.

Amidst this struggle, the revelation of my father's similar marks came later in my teenage years. The dermatologist's inquiry unearthed a family connection to these distinctive marks. It was a revelation that shed light on the genetic aspect of my condition, an aspect that had been concealed from me until then.

As I coped with the physical and emotional challenges posed by the marks, life unfolded with both unpleasant and poignant experiences. The desire to wear makeup, a means to alleviate the emotional toll, was met with resistance from family members who deemed me too young. The conflict reached a head at my grandmother's house, where familial opinions clashed over whether I should be allowed to wear makeup.

This desire to use makeup as a form of self-expression and confidence clashed with societal judgments. The first time I ventured into the world wearing makeup was met with ridicule from peers. Their taunts and laughter served as a stark reminder that no matter the effort to conceal the marks or enhance my appearance, the judgment persisted.

In my high school years, I faced a difficult time as my classmates made fun of my makeup, calling my face "dead" and "too pale." It was a challenging period for me, as I found myself caught between societal expectations and my attempts at self-expression. This experience left a lasting impression on me, as it taught me the harsh realities of societal pressures and how they can affect one's sense of self.

Throughout this journey, my relationship with my older sister, Ariana, provided moments of solace. Despite the significant age gap, she embraced the role of a supportive big sister. Her excitement at the prospect of becoming a sibling was palpable, and her departure for outings triggered my tearful desire to follow in her footsteps.

As I moved through these formative years, grappling with societal judgments and familial conflicts, my sister Ariana stood as a pillar of support. In the intricate tapestry of my childhood, she played a role that extended beyond the visible marks on my face, offering a sense of connection and understanding in a world that often seemed unsympathetic.

When I was young, Hurricane Katrina hit us hard and changed our lives completely. We had to leave behind our home in New Orleans and move to Texas and then Arkansas. The hurricane devastated the area and disrupted our daily routine. It was a significant event during my childhood that I will never forget.

The decision to evacuate was influenced by my uncle Tyrone, who foresaw the impending danger. Reluctantly, we left our home, seeking refuge in Texas, only to find the solace we sought elusive. Texas offered little reprieve, prompting a move to Arkansas, where a homeless shelter became a temporary haven for my family. The shelter, a makeshift dwelling, witnessed our shared moments of uncertainty and resilience.

In Arkansas, life took on a new rhythm. The school environment, markedly different from the one back in New Orleans, brought a sense of acceptance. The kids were kinder, the teachers more accommodating. Surprisingly, I found myself excelling academically, escaping the confines of special education classes. The policies in Arkansas allowed me to join regular classes, where I thrived, earning grades that brought a newfound sense of accomplishment.

As I embraced this period of stability in Arkansas, my cousins, children of my aunt Ursula, struggled with the displacement. They yearned for a swift return to New Orleans, often shuttling back and forth to hasten the reconstruction process. However, each return to New Orleans left me with a sense of melancholy, as I had grown attached to the sense of belonging, I found in Arkansas.

Friendships blossomed in Arkansas, offering a respite from the judgment I had experienced in New Orleans. Kids were kind, and compliments replaced the taunts that had once haunted me. My academic achievements became a source of pride, a testament to the resilience that defined our journey.

Yet, despite the newfound stability, the yearning for New Orleans persisted within my family. Home, with its intricate ties to family and familiarity, remained a magnetic force drawing us back. Arkansas, as much as I cherished the friendships and the academic progress, couldn't replace the sense of rootedness that only our New Orleans home could provide.

Returning to New Orleans marked a bittersweet homecoming. The familiar hallways of my previous school, though tinged with memories of ridicule and judgment, served as a backdrop to my reentry into the city. Despite the challenges, Arkansas had bestowed upon me a newfound resilience, and a determination to navigate the turbulent waters of my adolescence.

The drive back to New Orleans mirrored the landscape of my emotions, a blend of sorrow for leaving behind newfound friends in Arkansas and trepidation for the resumption of the familiar battles in my hometown. As the cityscape unfolded before me, I couldn't shake the yearning for the sense of acceptance I had found in the Arkansas classrooms.

The return to New Orleans didn't offer the solace I sought. The taunts, the isolation, and the challenges of special education classes resumed with a disheartening familiarity. The harsh reality of the post-Katrina landscape hit me anew when I walked into our once-flooded house. The devastation, the loss, and the destruction of everything we had known left an indelible mark on my soul.

Yet, amidst the ruins, my mother's comforting words echoed, reassuring me that we would rebuild. Hurricane Katrina, a catastrophic force that reshaped the city, became a defining phase, a narrative thread woven into the fabric of my early years. The return to New Orleans, though fraught with challenges, also symbolized a resilience that mirrored the city's spirit.

Growing up in New Orleans was like navigating through a symphony of flavors and traditions. While pancake breakfasts formed the staple of my childhood diet due to financial constraints, my grandmother's house became a haven for indulging in culinary delights. Gumbo, seafood, grits, eggs, and the tantalizing aroma of fried shrimp and fish painted a vivid picture of the diverse and mouthwatering culinary landscape that New Orleans had to offer.

My early years were marked by the juxtaposition of limited means at home and a culinary extravaganza at my grandmother's. The holidays were a particularly cherished time, when the entire family congregated at my grandmother's house to share laughter, stories, and, of course, the delectable feast that was spread before us. Mardi Gras, with its vibrant parades and the excitement of catching beads, added another layer of joy to my childhood memories.

The warmth of the neighborhood further enriched my upbringing. In New Orleans, everyone seemed to know everyone. My mother's friendly exchanges with neighbors created a sense of community where people looked out for each other. This interconnectedness extended to me, as the watchful eyes of neighbors made me feel like part of an extended family whether it was a casual greeting or a friendly reminder from a neighbor that they had seen me outside, the sense of familiarity and safety was deeply ingrained in the fabric of our community.

Despite the challenges that later unfolded in my teenage years, the foundation of a supportive community during my childhood was a source of comfort. The neighbors' watchful eyes weren't just about surveillance; they were a manifestation of a shared responsibility and concern for one another. In this tightly-knit neighborhood, safety wasn't just a concept; it was a palpable reality that allowed me to explore, play, and grow with a sense of security.

As the seasons changed, and the festivities of Mardi Gras gave way to the tranquility of everyday life, the beauty of New Orleans became apparent in its unique blend of culture, community, and cuisine. The city's allure wasn't just in its famous celebrations but also in the day-to-day interactions that shaped my formative years.

However, the idyllic scenes of my childhood stood in stark contrast to the challenges that awaited me as I entered my teenage years. The watchful eyes of the neighbors, once a comforting presence, took on a different hue as adolescence brought with it a heightened sense of scrutiny and judgment. This transition marked a turning point in my relationship with the community that had been my anchor, setting the stage for the complexities of my high school journey.

Chapter 3:
The Ever-Silent Parent

During my teenage years, attending Joseph S. Clark High School was a significant part of my journey. Without the means of transportation, my Auntie Ursula was kind enough to shuttle me to and from school every day. This routine was essential, as it connected my home life to my education.

Upon arriving at the school, we went through security checks to ensure that no weapons or prohibited items could enter the premises. The metal detector hummed as it scanned us, reminding us of the need for vigilance in the educational environment. Once cleared, we made our way through the hallways to attend regular and special education classes.

In the realm of academics, I found myself straddling two worlds. My mornings began in regular homeroom classes, where I immersed myself in the ebb and flow of typical school routines. English classes, with their syllabi and literature, offered a glimpse into the mainstream academic experience. However, the threads of my education began to weave into a tapestry of contrast.

When I was in high school, I had to attend special education classes due to my unique learning needs. This meant that I had to leave my regular class and go to a different classroom, which sometimes caused my classmates to look at me curiously. It made me feel self-conscious and as though I was standing out negatively. The transition from regular classes to special education classes sometimes felt like the hallway itself was a stage that highlighted the differences in our educational paths.

I received special education, also known as "special ed," which helped me with my academic challenges through customized approaches. These classes were designed for students who require an individualized education plan (IEP). They offered a more personalized and supportive learning environment, which was crucial for my academic growth. My regular teachers provided work to help me, but the collaboration with special education teachers played a vital role in my educational journey.

My high school routine involved navigating both regular and special education classes. While leaving a regular class for special education often came with a silent stigma, it was a path that aimed to provide an inclusive education tailored to my needs. This duality was an important part of my experience.

During my time in special education classes, I experienced more than just academic learning. The supportive community that formed within those classrooms provided a sense of belonging and understanding. Students with varying challenges shared their silent struggles, creating meaningful connections that went beyond the academic curriculum.

As I went through different academic transitions, I realized that my mother played a minimal role in my school life. While other parents actively engaged with teachers and attended school events, my mother remained elusive. Her absence during parent-teacher meetings and school functions left a silent void that was louder than any words could convey.

I found myself caught between regular and special education classes. I have to admit that being in the special education environment was different. Teachers would often provide answers to assignments, making our learning process simpler. This resulted in us copying down solutions without really understanding how to solve the problems.

When I think back on my experience in special education classes, I can't help but notice how easily it was to confuse true comprehension with simply following instructions. The environment in those classes was a mix of friendship and academic shortcuts, which highlighted the non-traditional path many of us were on. We navigated our education with a unique set of challenges that required flexibility and resilience.

During my time in special education classes, I always felt like I didn't quite fit in. Seeing the diversity of challenges faced by my classmates made me question whether the label "special education" really captured the unique experiences each student had in the classroom.

Although there were some moments of camaraderie, my high school experience was mostly marked by isolation. Some of my classmates, perhaps struggling with their insecurities, took it upon themselves to single me out. They taunted and teased me, fueled by misconceptions and stereotypes, making me an easy target. Nonetheless, I remained strong, avoiding physical confrontations and navigating the social dynamics with quiet determination.

As I got older, I started experimenting with makeup like many teenagers do. Unfortunately, this led to even more unwanted attention.

I remember the day I decided to wear makeup and experiment with the transformative artistry that many of my peers were exploring. However, I was not prepared for the negative reactions that followed. As I walked into school with a touch of makeup, I faced judgmental glances and taunts. People around me were surprised and made hurtful comments like "You got makeup on!" This made me feel vulnerable since adolescence is already a challenging period.

I felt the weight of being different more acutely. One day, a girl whose name I can't recall, made a cruel comment about my appearance, using derogatory terms that hurt me deeply. It was a moment of realization that highlighted the harsh judgments teenagers impose, as they grapple with their insecurities.

To avoid further ridicule, I focused on retreating from the public gaze and avoiding judgmental eyes. The classroom became both my sanctuary and battleground, where I pursued education while also facing the silent struggles of adolescence. This phase of my life involved more than just academic pursuits. It was a time when I was negotiating my identity while also building resilience to shield myself from social scrutiny.

During my time in high school, there was an incident that remains vivid in my memory. It involves a natural biological process that most people keep to themselves. At school, we wore light-colored khaki pants as part of our uniform. Unfortunately, when my period arrived unexpectedly, it turned into an embarrassing situation. I felt ashamed and uncomfortable when I realized that there was blood on the back of my pants. I had to go to the nurse's office, and my mother had to step in to help me save some of my dignity.

A surprising friendship blossomed in high school that went beyond the usual social norms of popularity and acceptance. It was based on a shared sense of being an outsider in a school where judgment was rampant. The two friends were not brought together by their mutual classes or acquaintances but by their experiences of feeling different from others. One girl, who had a darker complexion, became an ally to the other in the halls of Joseph S. Clark High School.

During my freshman days, I made friends with someone whose name I couldn't quite remember. We connected because we were both struggling to navigate the complexities of adolescence and high school's social scene. She had also experienced loneliness, and we found solace in each other's company. As we shared our stories, she introduced me to chat lines, where people could connect through virtual rooms using a 1-800 number. This concept piqued my adolescent curiosity, and I was intrigued by the idea of connecting with others beyond the physical confines of school.

Her generous offer to share this mysterious chat line number marked a pivotal moment in my freshman year. The notion of connecting with others beyond the stifling walls of high school ignited a spark of excitement. In a time when smartphones were not yet ubiquitous, the chat line provided a unique avenue for communication. The intrigue grew, and one evening, I decided to venture into this uncharted territory.

Dialing the 1-800 number, I was greeted by a cacophony of voices—strangers sharing snippets of their lives in a chaotic symphony. It was an auditory collage, with conversations overlapping and intertwining. Navigating through the labyrinth of virtual rooms, each designated by symbols, I glimpsed a novel form of interaction.

The allure of anonymity and the promise of connections propelled me forward. In a crowded room of voices, I stumbled upon an encounter that stood out—a conversation with a guy named Ty. As our virtual dialogue unfolded, he posed the standard questions—name, location, and age. In the realm of the chat line, honesty became negotiable, and I chose to conceal the vulnerabilities of adolescence behind a fabricated age.

In the glow of my dimly lit room, our virtual connection with Ty blossomed. What began as a chance encounter on the chat line evolved into a daily exchange of messages, punctuating the routine of my high school days. As I navigated the tumultuous halls of Joseph S. Clark High School, Ty's morning greetings became a source of solace, a digital ray of sunshine in the often-stormy landscape of adolescence.

Our conversations transcended the superficiality of teenage interactions within the school's walls. Ty, residing in Miami, and I, a high school freshman in New Orleans, forged a connection that defied the constraints of geography. It was a friendship that unfolded in the ethereal space of virtual rooms, free from the judgmental gaze of our peers.

Ty, seemingly unfazed by the fact that I was still navigating the complexities of adolescence, inquired about my life outside school walls. Faced with the question of employment, I conjured an imaginary job at a hotel—an occupation plucked from my sister's experiences. In the realm of the chat line, embellishing details became a playful dance, a way to present an idealized version of oneself.

The initial conversations gradually expanded beyond the boundaries of casual banter. Ty's genuine interest in my day-to-day life fostered a sense of connection, providing a comforting contrast to the challenges faced within the physical realm of high school. The routine exchanges of "Good morning" and "How's your day going?" assumed a profound significance, acting as digital lifelines that tethered us across the miles.

Amid the echoes of classroom chatter, the buzz of my phone signified a portal to a world where judgments were suspended, and the strains of teenage conformity were momentarily lifted. Ty's messages became a beacon, cutting through the noise of high school drama and adolescent insecurities. It was a respite—a connection that felt authentic in its simplicity.

As our virtual friendship deepened, Ty and I found solace in each other's company. The seemingly mundane details of our lives became the threads weaving the fabric of our connection. From the small triumphs to the challenges we faced, the chat line served as a digital confessional where vulnerabilities could be shared without fear of judgment.

As my friendship with Ty progressed, the lines between reality and the virtual realm blurred. Our connection deepened, accompanied by the inevitable twist of him expressing the desire to be my boyfriend. The digital dialogue took a turn into uncharted territories, and in the echo of a phone call, we tentatively agreed to embark on this virtual relationship.

Ty, who had initially presented himself as a 26-year-old from Miami, began sharing more about his life. A car wash employee with family struggles, he unfolded a narrative of challenges and resilience. The virtual space became a canvas where we painted idealized versions of our lives, each layer more embellished than the last.

Yet, the essence of our relationship remained rooted in a shared understanding—both of us grappling with the complexities of life, seeking solace in the virtual companionship we had stumbled upon. Ty's voice became a familiar presence in the soundtrack of my teenage days, weaving through the fabric of my everyday experiences.

However, beneath the façade of this burgeoning connection lay the intricacies of my adolescent mind. Fueled by a desire for acceptance and understanding, I resorted to a curious strategy. Ty had requested pictures of me, and rather than revealing my true self, I resorted to using images of women from magazines and books, presenting an altered reality.

These images became the currency of our virtual bond—fragments of a narrative that teetered on the edge of fiction. Ty, seemingly aware but choosing not to confront the charade, played along. The intricacies of my teenage insecurities wove a tapestry of deception, with each shared image becoming a brushstroke in a portrait of make-believe.

As our conversations unfolded, a peculiar pattern emerged—Ty's possessiveness. Initially a refuge from the tribulations of high school, the digital realm became a stage for his insecurities. The imaginary man in my life became a source of conflict, casting a shadow over the authenticity we had cultivated.

Late-night calls turned into confrontations, with Ty convinced that a male presence lingered in the background. The intensity of these accusations escalated, revealing the fragility of our virtual connection. Each assertion of my innocence met with skepticism, and Ty's doubts began to unravel the carefully crafted fabric of our digital companionship.

Amid these storms, my high school friend, the one who had introduced me to the chat line, sensed the turmoil. She questioned the authenticity of Ty's age and expressed concern about the tumultuous nature of our virtual relationship. As a teenager navigating uncharted territories, I defended the connection, rationalizing away the complexities that unfolded beneath the surface.

Ty's reaction to this disruption was profound—a manifestation of the fragility of our digital thread. The house phone, the last bastion of our communication, became a lifeline he clung to desperately. The unraveling of our virtual connection mirrored the tumultuous emotions of adolescence, leaving me to grapple with the remnants of a relationship that transcended the confines of both the physical and digital worlds.

Chapter 4:
Crossing Lines for Connection

Ty and I had a virtual relationship that gradually became blurry. We talked mostly at night and kept it secret. However, things changed when my mother discovered our conversations. One day, as we were talking on the phone, my mother picked it up and heard Ty's voice. She was surprised to learn that he was my boyfriend. They had a conversation while I was bewildered.

This marked the first time my family confronted the tangible existence of Ty, a character who had until then only existed within the confines of my phone. My mother, grappling with this unexpected revelation, sought answers from me. Questions echoed through the room—Who is he? How old is he? What does he want with my daughter?

When I was in either the 10th or 11th grade, I struggled to explain to my mother who Ty was. I told her he was a friend who lived out of town. However, when I mentioned that he was 26 years old, she became worried and skeptical. The situation was confusing for her, as she was both concerned for my safety and unsure how to handle this aspect of our digital relationship.

Once the phone confiscation saga ended, my mother returned my phone, and with it came a flood of unanswered texts and missed calls from Ty. The virtual turmoil continued as he sought explanations for my perceived silence. On the other end of the line, Ty's intensity oscillated between accusations and apologies, a cycle fueled by his insecurities and an expressed fondness for me.

Attempting to quell Ty's suspicions, I concocted lies about being with another man—an intricate web of deception spun to maintain a precarious balance. The fragility of our digital connection, laid bare during the phone confiscation incident, left me contemplating the complexities of teenage relationships in both the physical and virtual realms.

Ty's remorseful texts followed, acknowledging the irrationality of his actions. He admitted that his fondness for me fueled his possessiveness, adding a layer of emotional vulnerability to our dynamic. The allure of meeting in person emerged, with Ty expressing a desire to bridge the physical gap that separated us. However, the prospect of real-world interaction raised questions about the feasibility and the implications of such a meeting.

In an attempt to nurture the relationship, I embarked on a peculiar journey of financial contributions. Fueled by my part-time job earnings and a budding affection for Ty, I accumulated a small fund, initially intended for my lunch. However, the significance of these funds transcended the realms of school meals—they became a lifeline connecting me to Ty's world.

There was a moment, a testament to the complexities of adolescence, where I managed to save up $500. This hard-earned money, symbolic of my teenage endeavors, found a different purpose when Ty reached out, narrating his financial hardships. Struggling after losing his job and facing eviction, Ty sought assistance. The request echoed through our digital conversations, underscoring the blurred lines between virtual connection and the tangible world.

Approaching my mother for assistance, I concocted a story about losing my ID to justify the funds being sent in her name. Unbeknownst to my family, I became a conduit of financial support for Ty, a testament to the intricate web of trust and dependence we had woven into our digital dialogue. My mother, though unaware of the underlying dynamics, agreed to facilitate this financial exchange.

The process of sending money unfolded, drawing attention from my aunt during a walk to the dollar store. Ty's incessant calls, fueled by jealousy and possessiveness, became a familiar soundtrack to my interactions with family. Each call painted a portrait of my isolation—his refusal to accept my presence with family members and constant suspicions about potential companionship. My aunt, observing this tumultuous dance, voiced her concerns, recognizing the abnormality of Ty's behavior.

In the realm of regular classes, a stark disparity arose. The intricacies of subjects eluded me, and comprehension felt like a distant goal. During an English class, the teacher called on me to read aloud—an endeavor fraught with anxiety due to my feet condition. The echoes of laughter from classmates lingered, a testament to the vulnerability that accompanies adolescence. The embarrassment seared into my memory, a reminder of my struggles within the confines of the traditional education system.

Amidst these challenges, a glimmer of hope arose when I entertained the possibility of graduating early. The prospect of an accelerated path to independence fueled my excitement. The idea of joining Ty sooner rather than later, escaping the constraints of high school life, beckoned as an appealing prospect. However, this hope faced a crushing blow when bureaucratic constraints revealed I had to wait another year due to mandatory classes.

Fueled by disappointment, I navigated this setback by immersing myself in extracurricular activities. The principal suggested joining the band or choir to fulfill the requirements for graduation. My foray into the band proved short-lived, but choir became a source of joy and self-expression. Singing alongside older students provided a respite from the challenges I faced in other aspects of school life.

Yet, even in the choir's harmonious melodies, the discord of my personal life persisted. The longing for Ty and the challenges of a long-distance relationship added an emotional layer to my high school experience. The principal's directive to take up an additional class left me yearning for the independence I craved.

In the choir, the interactions with older students brought a different dynamic. Their indifference was a peculiar form of solace, providing a brief respite from the incessant attention or mockery I had experienced in previous classes. The dichotomy between being ignored and being teased left me questioning the nature of acceptance I sought.

The disappointment of not graduating on time weighed heavily on me, and the artifice of a future reunion with Ty became a distant dream. Communicating this delay to Ty, I felt the burden of our long-distance relationship intensify. Despite the challenges, I sought solace in the choir's harmonious melodies and occasional field trips.

Back home, my mother's reluctance to advocate for me to join regular classes became a source of confusion and frustration. My Auntie Ursula's influence played a role in the decision, leaving me perplexed about my mother's perspective. Conversations with my mother about this echoed the sentiment of familial love overriding individual aspirations.

Initially, Ty had reservations about making it to our meeting. He cited fatigue from work and lack of transportation. Faced with the possibility of our anticipated reunion falling apart, my emotions ran high. I considered abandoning the plan altogether, finding myself in the kitchen, expressing my reluctance to my mother.

However, a call from Ty that night shifted the narrative. His apology and reassurance swayed my decision, reigniting the spark of excitement for the impending journey. The complexities of our long-distance relationship came to the forefront, but optimism prevailed, and I conveyed the details of our upcoming visit to Ty.

Upon arrival in Miami, the city embraced us with its vibrant energy. Ty's apartment, a small refuge in the city, was my destination. The moment our eyes met in person; an unspoken understanding passed between us. The discrepancies in age and appearance that had lingered in the back of my mind dissipated. Instead, a genuine connection emerged as he complimented me without any mention of the manipulated images from our past conversations.

As we delved into the conversation, the uncertainty about Ty's age lingered. Despite my concerns, Ty's demeanor and the mutual comfort between us overshadowed the need for explicit discussions about age. We spent time exploring the city, going to the mall across the street, and immersing ourselves in conversation.

However, our meeting wasn't devoid of external commentary. The roommate at Ty's apartment, an older man with limited English proficiency, observed our interaction and inquired if I was Ty's girlfriend. Ty, in response, simply shook his head, creating an air of mystery around our connection. As we retreated to Ty's room, the roommate's subtle gestures hinted at his approval.

Navigating this newfound proximity with Ty brought about a mix of emotions. His apartment became a haven where the complexities of our relationship unfolded. The age difference, which had caused me considerable anxiety, seemed inconsequential in the face of the connection we shared.

With my mother and Auntie Pam stationed at the hotel, the notion of having personal space with Ty felt liberating. Yet, a sense of caution lingered, with my family ensuring they had Ty's contact details, underscoring the protective measures in place.

The initial days were filled with both optimism and challenges. Despite the absence of a physical relationship, Ty's growing paranoia about other men in the vicinity became a noticeable strain. His anxiety intensified when he wasn't around, revealing a vulnerability that I hadn't fully grasped during our long-distance communication.

Our connection was defined by conversations rather than physical intimacy. I candidly shared my status as a virgin, expressing my reluctance to engage in such matters at that point in our relationship. Ty, understanding and supportive, assured me that our bond went beyond physicality. This mutual understanding strengthened the emotional aspect of our connection.

Amidst the challenges, the idea of having our place emerged as a solution to Ty's paranoia. Securing an apartment in the same complex where my mother and grandmother resided became a pivotal moment in our journey. This newfound independence allowed us to navigate the intricacies of our relationship without external influences.

However, the financial aspect presented a hurdle. At the time, my disability payments were directed to my grandmother. Taking a bold step towards independence, I approached my mother to request a change in the arrangement. I wanted my disability funds to be directed to me directly. While rooted in the desire for autonomy, this decision had implications for my family members who relied on those funds.

The transition into adulthood, marked by financial autonomy and cohabitation, revealed the complexities of our situation. As we carved out a space for ourselves, my family grappled with the changes, both in my individual choices and in the dynamics of our collective support system.

The months passed, and the routine of our daily lives settled in. Ty continued to work, and I found solace in moments when we could share our thoughts and dreams. The absence of a conventional high school experience and the challenges I faced earlier were momentarily eclipsed by the possibilities of a future with Ty.

Yet, the echoes of my family's concerns reverberated. They had urged me to return home, to complete my last year of high school, a plea that echoed in phone calls from my mother, grandmother, sister, and uncle. The weight of their disappointment pressed upon me, and I realized that I had let them down.

The prospect of finishing my education in Miami, far from the familiarity of home, became a point of contention. I grappled with the desire for independence and the understanding that my family yearned for me to complete the journey I had started in New Orleans.

As the days unfolded in Miami, the dynamics of my relationship with Ty continued to shift. Despite the hurdles we faced, we navigated life together in our small apartment. Ty, working under the table, sustained us with cash, and we settled into a routine.

One day, Ty's job-related paranoia surfaced unexpectedly. He took me to the car wash to meet his co-workers, a seemingly harmless introduction. However, misunderstandings arose when he thought I had given my number to a male co-worker. This misconception led to a fight, resulting in Ty losing his job. The financial strain intensified, directing most of my disability funds towards bills.

Money became tight, and our daily routine settled into a monotonous pattern. I contemplated returning to school, initially telling Ty about my desire to attend college, omitting the fact that I needed to finish high school first. However, Ty was not supportive of the idea, assuming ulterior motives.

Our apartment was in a higher-priced area, providing convenient access to hair salons and nail shops. However, I faced challenges finding professionals who understood how to care for Black textured hair. The language barrier in the neighborhood, primarily Spanish-speaking, compounded the difficulties of daily life.

Despite the occasional outing to Miami Beach and grocery shopping, my sense of isolation grew. Ty's possessiveness manifested in discomfort during public outings, further contributing to my feeling trapped. As the months passed, the routine became suffocating, leading to a momentous decision.

On my 19th birthday, the pressure for a sexual relationship reached its peak. Ty, pushing for intimacy, highlighted the passage of a year in our relationship. Despite my hesitations, we engaged in a physical relationship, marking a shift in our connection.

The relationship took another unexpected turn when Ty suggested a threesome after watching a TV show. Navigating the complexities of such an arrangement, we found a woman named JoJo on an app. The experience, however, turned painful when she expressed discomfort, and Ty's actions left me deeply hurt.

The aftermath of the threesome marked a turning point. Emotionally wounded and mentally done, I grappled with the desire to return home and the fear of facing judgment from my family. Despite the internal turmoil, I resolved to stand up for myself, asserting my right to maintain contact with my family.

A chance encounter with Kevin, while seeking permission to spend $5, opened a door to a different possibility. Kevin, respectful of my relationship but sensing my vulnerability, offered a connection outside the confines of my strained partnership with Ty.

Chapter 5:
Unexpected Connections

As I strolled to the corner store, intending to grab a drink, a chance encounter altered the course of my story. Kevin, a stranger, held the door for me. He struck up a conversation, introducing himself and expressing interest in getting to know me. Hesitant but open to making friends, I agreed to exchange numbers.

Upon returning home, Kevin wasted no time in calling. We arranged to meet at a nearby restaurant where, right away, I laid out the complexities of my life—my boyfriend Ty, the sense of isolation, and the challenges I faced. Kevin, 22 years old, had recently been released on parole and coincidentally lived in the same apartment complex.

Our friendship developed quickly. Kevin, aware of my daily routines, offered companionship during my off-hours. He became a confidant, listening to my concerns about Ty and providing a different perspective. His own experiences, having been in a program after incarceration, added a layer of understanding to our conversations.

Despite his two roommates' initial disapproval, Kevin and I spent time together watching TV and talking. The roommates, older men themselves, questioned my presence, aware of my relationship with Ty. But Kevin defended our friendship, asserting that it was none of their business.

In a way, Kevin became a refuge from the complexities of my relationship with Ty. His straightforwardness and willingness to listen provided a sense of comfort. It was a friendship that started innocently, offering me a reprieve from the emotional turbulence that had marked my time in Miami.

As days turned into weeks, Kevin's presence in my life grew more significant. He expressed genuine concern about my well-being, often urging me to reconsider my situation with Ty. His perspective, shaped by his own life experiences, offered a fresh lens through which to view my circumstances.

The contrasts between Ty and Kevin became more evident. While Ty's possessiveness created an isolating environment, Kevin encouraged independence and self-reflection. As Kevin's influence grew, I found myself contemplating my choices and questioning the direction of my life.

One evening, as Kevin and I sat at his place, he raised a topic that sparked introspection. He encouraged me to consider my goals, aspirations, and what I truly wanted from life. This conversation planted seeds of self-discovery, prompting me to think beyond the constraints of my current situation.

Despite the challenges and uncertainties that lay ahead, Kevin emerged as an unexpected anchor. His friendship became a source of strength, offering support and encouragement as I navigated the complexities of relationships, personal growth, and the pursuit of a life that felt authentic to me.

As time passed, Kevin and I continued to spend a lot of time together in his room. He often invited me to various events, attempting to introduce me to a different side of Miami. I remember one instance when he suggested we attend a concert featuring Nicki Minaj.

Excited about the idea, I regretfully declined due to my responsibilities and the late-night schedule, which seemed to disappoint him.

Our friendship grew deeper, providing me with an escape from the complexities of my relationship with Ty. Kevin seemed to understand the challenges I faced and offered companionship without judgment. Despite the initial reservations of his roommates, our bond remained steadfast.

One significant chapter in our journey unfolded on Valentine's Day. Eager to surprise Ty, I prepared a special evening, adorned in lingerie and with a homemade dinner. However, the atmosphere quickly soured when Ty returned home with an inexplicably off mood. Accusing me of wanting the attention of an old man living across the street, Ty unleashed his anger, making baseless allegations about my intentions. The incident left me in tears, confused and hurt by the unwarranted accusations.

Amidst these turbulent moments, Kevin became a source of solace. He listened to my frustrations, providing support and understanding. As our friendship deepened, he encouraged me to reevaluate my situation with Ty and contemplate what I truly desired from life.

The emotional strain in my relationship with Ty continued, marked by instances of possessiveness and unfounded accusations. Despite these challenges, I grappled with the fear of returning home, knowing the judgment I might face from my family. This fear, coupled with a lack of financial independence, kept me tethered to a situation that was becoming increasingly toxic.

As the days unfolded, I found myself at a crossroads, torn between the comfort of the familiar and the allure of the unknown. Kevin's friendship became a guiding light, encouraging me to reassess my goals and aspirations. He shared stories of his struggles, demonstrating that life could be different.

During this internal struggle, an unexpected opportunity presented itself. Kevin, aware of my desire to explore beyond the confines of my current situation, proposed a daring idea. He suggested a road trip—an escape from the routine and a chance to experience life outside the confines of Miami.

This proposition ignited a spark within me. The prospect of breaking free from the suffocating dynamics of my relationship with Ty and embarking on a journey of self-discovery held an undeniable appeal. The road trip, with its promise of new beginnings, symbolized a path toward independence and autonomy.

In the aftermath of that disheartening Valentine's Day, I found myself questioning the nature of my relationship with Ty. Love, I thought, shouldn't be marked by tears and unwarranted accusations. The emotional toll was taking its toll on me, and I confided in Kevin about the turmoil at home.

Kevin, ever supportive, affirmed that I deserved better. His encouragement to reconsider my situation and pursue personal growth resonated with me. As our friendship deepened, I began to see him as a source of solace—a friend who cared about my well-being.

In a candid moment, I admitted my growing fondness for Kevin, and to my relief, he reciprocated the sentiment. Our connection deepened, culminating in a moment of intimacy. However, the weight of guilt and betrayal clouded my emotions, prompting a tearful departure from Kevin's place.

Returning home to Ty, I grappled with conflicting feelings. The emotional distance between Ty and me was growing, but a sense of obligation kept me tethered to the facade of normalcy. I navigated the complexities of sleeping with Kevin during the day and Ty at night, not out of desire for Ty, but rather to avoid the confrontations and accusations that awaited me otherwise.

I confided in my mother about Kevin, but her concerns mirrored Ty's accusations. The complexity of my situation kept me from sharing the full extent of Ty's mental and emotional abuse. The strain on my relationship with my mother increased, leading to a gradual withdrawal from sharing the intricacies of my life.

Despite these challenges, Kevin became a sanctuary—a place where I could escape the turbulence at home. His encouragement to focus on personal growth, echoed by the opportunities he presented, sparked the idea of a road trip. The prospect of a journey with Kevin, away from the confines of Miami, promised a chance for self-discovery and independence.

I continued juggling my complicated relationships with Ty and Kevin while grappling with unexpected news—I was pregnant. The revelation filled me with mixed emotions; the prospect of having a child excited me, yet it also signaled a seismic shift in my life.

Unsure of the paternity, I first confided in Kevin, thinking that the baby might be his. His reaction was surprisingly positive, expressing joy at the idea of becoming a father. He envisioned a future together, even suggesting talking to his case manager to explore the possibility of us getting a place of our own.

However, I hesitated, feeling that Kevin's eagerness to fast-track our relationship might be premature. I conveyed my concerns, emphasizing the need to take things slow and get to know each other better before making such significant decisions.

In an attempt to navigate this intricate web, I sought guidance from my mother, making her the second person I informed about my pregnancy. Over the phone, I shared the news, knowing she would have strong opinions on the matter. As our conversation unfolded, my mother urged caution, advising against rushing into major life changes.

Amidst the uncertainty, my primary focus was on my unborn child. The impending arrival prompted introspection, forcing me to evaluate the environment in which I wanted my child to grow. The toxic dynamics with Ty and the growing emotional connection with Kevin posed a dilemma—a choice that would profoundly impact the trajectory of my life as a mother.

My Auntie Pam, sensing my uncertainty about raising a child, suggested I return to New Orleans, where family support could guide me through the challenges of motherhood. On the phone, we deliberated about this possibility, weighing the pros and cons.

Amidst this, my mother expressed her desire for me to come back home. She believed that raising my baby in a familiar environment surrounded by family would provide a stable foundation. Their words resonated, but the decision remained complex.

Torn between the guidance of my aunt and the pull of familial ties, I contemplated my next steps. Meanwhile, Ty, unaware of the uncertainty clouding my mind, came home one night in an inebriated state. I braved the conversation, revealing the pregnancy test results. His initial shock gave way to acceptance, and he began envisioning the changes the baby would bring—talks of cribs and rearranging our lives together.

My mother's decision to visit Miami further complicated the situation. As we discussed the impending visit, the weight of my choices hung heavily. With Ty embracing the idea of impending fatherhood, my inner conflict deepened.

During this emotional turmoil, Kevin accompanied me to the doctor's appointment for confirmation. The news of a one-month pregnancy brought a mix of emotions, and I had an intuitive feeling it was a boy. Despite the excitement, I recognized that becoming a parent meant making significant life changes.

As the holiday season approached, my mother extended an invitation for Ty and me to spend Christmas or Thanksgiving in New Orleans. Reflecting on the chaos between Ty and Kevin, I saw it as an opportunity to step away and contemplate the path I wanted for myself and my unborn child.

My return to New Orleans carried a mix of emotions—I needed distance from both Kevin and Ty. While Ty declined the invitation to join me, my mother eagerly welcomed me back, expressing her joy at the prospect of having me home. Despite Ty's absence, I embarked on the journey alone, hoping for the support and clarity I sought.

Arriving at my family's home, I sensed a positive atmosphere initially. My mother, Auntie Pam, and the rest of the family embraced me with open arms, showering me with the warmth I needed. However, the positive vibes soon took a turn.

During a family gathering, with my sister on the phone on speaker, they assumed I was elsewhere in the house. As their conversation unfolded, I couldn't escape the negative energy that emerged. The joyful reunion started to feel strained as discussions delved into my life choices and the complexities of the relationships with Ty and Kevin.

Feeling exposed and vulnerable, I grappled with the weight of judgment and unsolicited advice. It became evident that even in the comfort of my family, I couldn't escape the challenges and scrutiny tied to my decisions.

As the holiday season progressed, the complexity of my situation unfolded against the backdrop of family dynamics and their well-intended but overwhelming opinions. The conflict between the support I craved and the judgments I faced intensified, forcing me to confront not only the challenges of my relationships but also the complexities of family expectations.

Feeling unsupported, I decided to return to Miami the next day, still uncertain about the path ahead. On the bus ride back, I pondered my options, torn between the conflicting advice from my family and the connections I had formed with Ty and Kevin.

Back in Miami, my mother suggested that I move back to New Orleans for financial support, emphasizing the challenges of raising a child without sufficient income. While I acknowledged the financial strain, I questioned the wisdom of returning to New Orleans and being reliant on Ty.

My mother decided to join me in Miami, not fully understanding the complexities of my relationships. Frustrated by her push for me to reunite with Ty and skeptical of his suitability as a father, I reluctantly allowed her to meet Kevin. Her disapproval of Kevin heightened the tension, but Kevin gracefully exited, sensing the need for a mother-daughter conversation.

My mother's persistent stance favored Ty, emphasizing his visual appeal over Kevin's youthfulness. Unbeknownst to her, Ty's appearance didn't align with societal standards either. The three-way dynamic remained complex, and my mother's opinions failed to capture the intricacies of my relationships with Ty and Kevin.

As tensions escalated, Kevin's frustration grew, emphasizing the challenges ahead due to his record hindering employment opportunities. The prospect of returning to New Orleans, where Ty was on parole, seemed unfavorable. Ty reluctantly agreed to let me go back home with my mother, planning to save up money and reunite once the baby arrived.

Our disagreements centered on the idea of getting an apartment together, a concept I wasn't ready to commit to. One night, under the guise of my mother covering for me, I met Kevin to share my decision to go back home. His reaction took a dark turn as he threatened to take the baby away, highlighting my lack of income and employment. Feeling cornered, he belittled me, using personal vulnerabilities I had confided in him against me.

The emotional weight of the situation intensified as Kevin manipulated my insecurities to control my choices. Hurt and confused, I stood my ground, asserting my right to keep my child. The power dynamic between us grew increasingly toxic, and I grappled with the realization that Kevin might not be the supportive partner I needed.

Meanwhile, my mother persistently tried to convince Ty to come to New Orleans, emphasizing the financial strain on Ty after my departure. Ty, however, was resistant, unsure about relocating to a city he knew little about, with no job prospects lined up. My mother, concerned about the financial implications, warned Ty about the challenges he would face alone.

Ty, contemplating a move to New Orleans, faced challenges due to a past altercation preventing him from getting a job. My mother, growing impatient with my indecision, took the initiative and booked her ticket back to New Orleans, leaving me alone in Miami.

Days passed, and my mother's departure forced me to confront the reality of my situation. I was torn between family drama, Ty's uncertain plans, and Kevin's manipulative behavior. The echoes of Kevin's hurtful words lingered, pushing me to reconsider my choices.

New Year's Eve arrived, and I spent it with Kevin, hoping to find clarity. The atmosphere was tense as Kevin, in a party mood, offered me a drink despite my pregnancy. The night turned into an argument as I insisted on discussing our future and the impending responsibilities of parenthood.

Amidst the clash of emotions, Kevin's reluctance to address the impending fatherhood became evident. Frustration mounted, and I stressed the need for him to mature and take responsibility. However, he seemed resistant, clinging to his carefree lifestyle. The realization struck that his priorities diverged from the serious commitment required for parenting.

This encounter marked my last attempt to salvage a sense of responsibility from Kevin. I confronted him, expressing my desire for him to be a father and urging him to grow up. The argument further highlighted our differences and Kevin's reluctance to transition into the responsibilities of parenthood.

Back in New Orleans, carrying the weight of my pregnancy and the emotional turmoil caused by Kevin, I sought refuge in the familiarity of family. The incident at IHOP had left me shaken, and the realization dawned that I needed guidance for the well-being of my unborn child.

Upon my return, Ty joined me in New Orleans, expressing a newfound commitment to be part of our baby's life. My mother, eager for stability and a support system, arranged living arrangements, giving Ty and me a space in the double house while she stayed nearby with my Auntie Pam.

As the months unfolded, Ty and I navigated the complexities of cohabitation. My mother and aunt, hopeful for a unified family, encouraged the relationship between Ty and me. Despite their efforts, the shadows of the past lingered, and my heart was torn between the desire for a stable family life and the haunting memories of Kevin's violent outburst.

The pregnancy progressed, and the preparations for the baby's arrival were in full swing. My emotions were a tumultuous mix of anticipation, fear, and uncertainty. I struggled with my own conflicting emotions about Ty and Kevin, and the looming responsibility of parenthood intensified the internal chaos.

Ty, committed to being a father, attended prenatal classes with me and showed genuine interest in the well-being of our child. Still, the memories of my time with Kevin lingered, and the fear of repeating past mistakes haunted me.

Chapter 6:
Embracing Change

In New Orleans, Ty and I settled into the house my mom arranged for us, a comforting space within a double house. My mom and Auntie Pam resided next door, creating a close-knit family environment. The support and stability offered by my family were a reassuring backdrop as we prepared for the impending arrival of our baby.

The financial dynamics shifted after Social Security cut off my SSI, leaving me without a personal income. My mom, taking charge of the household expenses, urged Ty and me to save for the baby's future. Despite the challenges, her guidance provided a sense of direction during this transitional period.

Ty's move to New Orleans marked a turning point, and I observed subtle changes in him. The paranoia that lingered from our time in Miami seemed to dissipate, and Ty appeared more at ease. Our connection deepened as we engaged in heartfelt conversations, addressing the complexities of our relationship, past hurts, and our shared journey into parenthood.

Navigating the nuances of cohabitation, Ty and I encountered both joys and challenges. The weight of past mistakes and the intricacies of our relationship cast shadows on our attempts to move forward. Despite my affection for Ty, the memories of our unconventional past continued to influence our interactions.

As the months unfolded, my mom, a constant pillar of support, emphasized the importance of financial prudence. Her reminders to save for the baby echoed in my mind, reinforcing the need for stability in life's uncertainties.

In the absence of my income, Ty and I relied on my mom's financial support. The responsibility of impending parenthood loomed large, and the realization that our decisions now impacted not only us but our unborn child added a layer of complexity to our relationship.

The social dynamics within our makeshift family prompted discussions about our future. The ever-present question of whether Ty was the right partner for a stable family life resurfaced. My mom and Auntie Pam, invested in the idea of a unified family, continued to encourage our relationship, hoping for a harmonious environment for the baby.

The process of self-discovery intertwined with the preparations for the baby's arrival. Ty's commitment to fatherhood shone through as he attended prenatal classes with me, displaying a genuine interest in our child's well-being. Despite the challenges, his willingness to engage in this shared journey offered glimmers of hope for a stable family life.

However, the shadows of our unconventional past lingered. The aftermath of the tumultuous threesome experience cast a long shadow on our relationship. Ty's effort to move forward collided with the weight of past mistakes, creating a delicate balance between progress and lingering doubts.

Amidst the tension, my dad's happiness about our presence provided a contrasting element. He genuinely welcomed us to New Orleans, creating a sense of joy in the challenges we faced within our household.

As Ty's dissatisfaction with our living arrangement continued, his comments about my family and their perceived noise levels grew more frequent. The strain on our relationship deepened, and discussions about his discomfort became a recurring theme. His desire for more privacy and autonomy clashed with the close-knit environment my family embraced.

Despite these challenges, the preparations for the baby's arrival pressed on. We attended doctor's appointments, shopped for baby essentials at the local dollar store, and made trips to Walmart for groceries. However, the looming tension made these outings less enjoyable, with Ty's discontent evident in his demeanor.

Ty's disapproval extended to my clothing choices, reflecting a growing strain in our communication. A simple disagreement about a pair of jeans highlighted the escalating conflicts within our relationship. As my due date approached, the weight of these unresolved issues cast a shadow over what should have been a time of shared excitement and anticipation.

The presence of my mom during our doctor visits became a point of contention for Ty. His desire for more privacy and fewer family members involved in our affairs clashed with my family's supportive nature. The delicate balance between Ty's expectations and the reality of my family's involvement became a recurring theme in our discussions.

The strains of our relationship also impacted our interactions with my sister's kids, keen and Destiny, who occasionally visited. Ty's concerns about noise levels and disruptions foreshadowed potential challenges once our baby arrived. The anticipation of becoming parents was overshadowed by Ty's dissatisfaction and the unresolved conflicts within our household.

The tension between Ty and my family reached its peak when it came to the birth of our baby boy. Ty, adamant about having exclusive time with the newborn, expressed his desire for no family members to be present at the hospital. This decision further strained the already delicate relationship between Ty and my family.

Despite my family's disappointment, I found myself caught in the middle. Ty insisted that I communicate his wishes to my family, creating a stressful dynamic. In an attempt to maintain peace, I asked my family to respect Ty's desire for a more private experience during this crucial moment.

As the due date approached, the atmosphere at home remained tense. The unresolved issues continued to cast a shadow over what should have been a joyous occasion. My family, respecting Ty's wishes, stayed away from the hospital, leaving me and Ty to navigate the birthing process alone.

The birth of our baby boy brought a mix of emotions. While the joy of becoming parents was undeniable, the strained relationships and Ty's control over the situation lingered in the background. The absence of my family during this significant moment reflected the deep-seated conflicts that had yet to be addressed.

Once we returned home with our newborn, the challenges persisted. Ty's desire for control extended to the baby's care and our daily routines. Any attempts by my family to offer assistance or support were met with resistance from Ty, reinforcing the growing divide between him and my loved ones.

The strain on our relationship and the challenges of co-parenting in this tense environment became increasingly apparent. Ty's need for control clashed with the familial support I sought, creating a continuous source of conflict. As we navigated the early days of parenthood, the unresolved issues from the past chapters continued to impact our present and future.

During these challenges, my family remained supportive, albeit from a distance. The desire for a harmonious family dynamic clashed with Ty's need for autonomy. Navigating this complex situation became a delicate balancing act, with the well-being of our newborn at the forefront of our concerns.

As our baby boy grew, so did the complexities of our co-parenting journey. The strain on our relationship with Ty persisted, creating an atmosphere of uncertainty and tension within our household. The challenges of parenting within this strained dynamic raised questions about the long-term viability of our relationship and the well-being of our growing family.

Before the baby arrived, there was a significant development. I decided to cut ties with Kevin for good. It was a necessary step to focus on making things work with Ty, as my family had expressed support for him. In what felt like a final conversation with Kevin, I forgave him for past transgressions and expressed my commitment to raising the baby in New Orleans.

Before the birth, we were living in my mom's house, and the decision to distance myself from Kevin was met with numerous phone calls from him. However, I stood my ground and maintained my resolve to build a life with Ty and our soon-to-arrive baby.

During this time, I needed to gather medical history for the baby, so I attempted to contact Kevin. Unfortunately, his phone was either disconnected or he had changed his number, making it impossible to reach him. With no way to reconnect, Kevin was officially out of the picture as I prepared for the arrival of my child.

As we settled into life in New Orleans, a new challenge emerged. Ty, who had control over our phone bill, would cut off my phone whenever he got upset with me. This became a regular occurrence, leaving me disconnected and wondering if Kevin was trying to reach out. Despite this, Ty's demeanor changed when he started smoking weed with neighbors around his age. It seemed to mellow him out, making him more pleasant and easier to be around. I found myself drawn to this altered version of Ty, appreciating the calmness that accompanied his highs.

Although I still believed Kevin might be the baby's father, Ty's presence and willingness to make things work for the sake of the child made me lean towards him. I was determined to provide my baby with a father figure, not wanting them to grow up without paternal support. At this point, Ty remained unaware of Kevin's existence, and I chose to focus on creating a stable environment for the impending arrival of our child.

While trying to make things work with Ty, I found myself still haunted by the trauma of what Kevin had done to me. The memories would creep into my thoughts, sometimes even in my dreams, causing me to wake up shaking. It was a weight I carried alone, as I had nobody to confide in about the dark experiences I had endured.

Ty's attempts to control the household and dictate terms to my mom and aunt strained our relationship.

He wasn't contributing financially, yet he wanted a say in how things were run. It created tension, and I struggled to maintain a sense of peace within the house. Meanwhile, I was still grappling with the aftermath of Kevin's mental and physical abuse.

As I reflected on the past, I realized I had internalized a lot of pain. Kevin's mental abuse lingered in my mind, and Ty's attempts at control added another layer of strain. Despite all this, I was determined to have a peaceful pregnancy and ensure the well-being of my unborn child.

One incident stood out during these challenging times. Ty joined me in New Orleans a few months after I had moved. The lady from the apartment complex informed me that Ty hadn't been paying rent. The apartment was in my name due to Ty's credit issues, and it turned out he hadn't contributed anything, damaging my credit in the process. Despite my efforts to explain the situation to the lady before leaving, Ty failed to keep his end of the deal, leaving me to deal with the consequences.

Despite Ty's promises of wanting to be present for the baby, it became evident that his motives might have been driven by financial struggles. His move to New Orleans seemed less about being a supportive father and more about seeking stability. Struggling in Miami, he likely realized he couldn't sustain the apartment and bills on his own, especially without my income.

My mom, in her generous spirit, offered him a place in New Orleans where he wouldn't have to worry about bills. She assured him that he could stay in the house without any financial obligations. This offer, coupled with the fact that he knew he couldn't manage on his own, prompted Ty's move to New Orleans.

So, I felt Ty's arrival in New Orleans was more about his struggles than a genuine desire to be part of our lives. His calls about financial difficulties signaled that he needed stability, and since he knew I was the source of income in Miami, he decided to join me in New Orleans. Despite my initial reservations, I told him to come because, deep down, I still cared for him.

However, I was aware that introducing Ty to my family and their dynamics might lead to drama. Throughout my time in Miami, I had avoided bringing Ty to visit my family, anticipating potential conflicts.

My intuition about the complications his arrival might cause proved correct.

There was an incident where I sent Ty a picture of my sister, and he insisted that she was the one texting him. It turned out he had obtained my sister's number from my phone without my knowledge. He sent inappropriate messages to her, assuming she had misled him about her identity in the pictures. This caused tension, but my sister never responded, and I confronted Ty about his actions.

So, the atmosphere in the house became increasingly awkward, especially on my auntie's side, as Ty's presence added a layer of tension. Interactions were strained, and my mom was caught in the middle, creating discomfort when we had to be in the same room together. The energy shifted, and it was clear that Ty's arrival had affected the family dynamic.

A particular incident involving my sister intensified the awkwardness. Ty, misunderstanding some pictures I sent him, assumed my sister had been texting him. This confusion led to an uncomfortable situation, with my sister avoiding interactions and my mom giving Ty disapproving looks. When I confronted Ty and clarified that I had sent the pictures, it eased the tension a bit, but the uneasiness lingered.

Despite these challenges, I pressed on, trying to create a semblance of normalcy. I asked Ty to respect my family and not involve them in any more misunderstandings. It was a tumultuous time, with the complications of relationships and misunderstandings adding stress to an already complex situation.

Chapter 7:
Without a Safety Net

When the time came for me to bring my first child into the world, it was a moment filled with both excitement and trepidation. Ty and I embarked on the journey to the hospital together, just the two of us. Despite the challenges we had faced in our relationship, there was a shared sense of anticipation as we prepared to welcome our little one.

As we arrived at the hospital, I couldn't shake the nerves that accompanied the impending labor. However, Ty's presence provided a source of comfort amidst the uncertainty. Together, we navigated the corridors of the hospital, ready to embrace whatever lay ahead.

The labor itself was a whirlwind of emotions. Despite the pain and intensity, there was a profound sense of joy knowing that soon I would hold my baby in my arms. And then, after what felt like an eternity, our son entered the world. Tyrone Christopher Coulter, a beautiful, healthy baby boy, filled the room with his cries, marking the beginning of a new phase in our lives.

In those precious moments after his birth, I felt a surge of overwhelming love and responsibility wash over me. This tiny bundle of joy was now my whole world, and I was determined to do everything in my power to ensure his happiness and well-being.

The days that followed were a blur of sleepless nights and endless diaper changes. Yet, amidst the exhaustion and chaos, there was a profound sense of contentment knowing that I was finally a mother. My family rallied around me, offering support and guidance as I navigated the challenges of early parenthood.

When we finally returned home from the hospital, our house was filled with a flurry of activity as friends and family came to meet the newest addition to our family. It was a joyous occasion, filled with laughter and love as we celebrated the arrival of our precious son.

However, amidst the celebrations, there were also moments of tension and disagreement. As a new mom, I found myself grappling with the realities of parenthood, while Ty seemed more preoccupied with his desires and interests. Instead of helping me with the baby, he often chose to spend his time socializing with neighbors, leaving me feeling overwhelmed and alone.

Adding to the stress was the constant scrutiny from my Auntie Pam. Despite her best intentions, her constant criticism only served to undermine my confidence as a mother. I found myself second-guessing every decision I made, afraid of making a mistake in her eyes.

One particular point of contention arose when Ty insisted on giving the baby water, despite my concerns. I had read extensively about newborn care and knew that giving water to a newborn could be dangerous. Yet, Ty dismissed my concerns, insisting that he knew best as the baby's father.

Our disagreement escalated into a heated argument, with neither of us willing to back down. In the end, Ty went against my wishes and gave the baby water behind my back. It was a betrayal of trust that left me feeling angry and resentful.

The consequences of his actions became apparent when the baby began experiencing stomach issues. Worried and anxious, we rushed him to the hospital, where the doctors confirmed that he had indeed been given too much water. It was a frightening experience that could have had serious repercussions for our baby's health.

In the aftermath of the incident, I couldn't help but feel a sense of betrayal. Despite my best efforts to protect our son, Ty disregarded my wishes and put him in harm's way. It was a stark reminder of the challenges we faced as new parents and the importance of communication and trust in a relationship.

As we returned home from the hospital, tensions ran high between us. I struggled to forgive Ty for his actions, while he seemed oblivious to the gravity of the situation. It was a difficult time for our relationship, as we grappled with the fallout from his decision.

Despite the challenges we faced, I remained determined to do what was best for my son. I sought solace in the love and support of my family, who stood by me through thick and thin. Together, we navigated the ups and downs of early parenthood, facing each challenge with courage and resilience.

Our arguments became more frequent as Ty continued to prioritize his interests over helping me with the baby. He would spend hours outside socializing with neighbors, seemingly oblivious to his responsibilities as a father. I found myself sitting on the porch, watching him from afar, feeling resentful and angry.

As the days passed, I noticed a shift in my demeanor. Simple tasks like doing my hair or getting my nails done no longer held the same appeal. I felt myself slipping into a state of depression, overwhelmed by the responsibilities of motherhood and the lack of support from Ty.

Despite the challenges, there were moments of reprieve when Ty would come home high and apologize for his behavior. He would offer to take care of the baby, giving me a much-needed break to attend to my own needs. These moments were rare but provided some semblance of relief amidst the chaos.

My relationship with my mom also became strained during this time. She struggled to understand our situation and often kept her distance, unsure of how to offer support. Instead, I found myself seeking solace in her presence, longing for the comfort of a mother's embrace.

Despite the challenges we faced, there were still moments of connection and intimacy between me and Ty. We shared tender moments as we navigated the trials of parenthood together, finding strength in each other's arms. But beneath the surface, there was a lingering sense of uncertainty about our future.

I began to question whether Ty was truly ready for the responsibilities of fatherhood or if his actions were driven more by his desires for stability and security. The doubts gnawed at me, fueling my insecurities and leaving me feeling adrift in a sea of uncertainty.

As the days passed, my niece and nephew began visiting more frequently, bringing their youthful energy into our home. One day, while they were over, they made some noise, as kids often do. Ty, already on edge, began fussing about the noise, his irritation palpable even through the thin walls separating our houses.

Their innocent chatter seemed to set him off, and he started making snide remarks about their noise levels. His frustration only escalated when they continued to make noise, and soon, his grumbling turned into full-blown anger.

I found myself caught in the middle, trying to diffuse the situation and calm Ty down. But his anger only intensified, and before I knew it, he stormed over to my Auntie Pam's side of the house.

I watched in shock as he confronted my nephew, King, shaking him roughly and demanding that he stop making noise. The sight of him manhandling a child sent chills down my spine, and I felt paralyzed, unsure of how to intervene.

Thankfully, my mom and auntie immediately stepped in, chastising Ty for his behavior and demanding that he leave the house. But Ty, stubborn as ever, refused to back down, insisting that he had every right to discipline my nephew.

The situation quickly escalated, with tensions running high and voices raised in anger. It was a chaotic scene, and I felt helpless as the situation spiraled out of control.

In the chaos, my auntie made a decision that would change everything. She called the police, seeking assistance in dealing with Ty's aggressive behavior. It was a drastic measure, but in that moment, it felt like the only option left to restore peace and order to our home.

As we waited for the police to arrive, the tension in the air was palpable. My heart raced with fear and uncertainty, unsure of what would happen next. But amidst the chaos, one thing became clear: our family was fractured, torn apart by anger and resentment.

In the aftermath of the incident, I found myself grappling with a whirlwind of emotions. I felt betrayed by Ty's actions, angry at his inability to control his temper. But beneath the anger, there was also a deep sense of sadness and disappointment, knowing that our once-close-knit family had been torn apart by violence and discord.

As we stood outside, grappling with the reality of our situation, the police arrived to assess the situation. They questioned us about whose house it was, and my mom bravely asserted that it was her house and that she didn't want Ty there. Amid the chaos, my Auntie Collette appeared out of nowhere, adding to the confusion and tension.

I couldn't forget the look on my mom's face—it was a mixture of sadness and disbelief as if she couldn't comprehend the turmoil unfolding before her eyes. Meanwhile, my auntie Pam was adamant that we had to leave, while the police reminded us that we were trespassing on the property.

With a sense of urgency, we hastily packed our belongings, including essentials for the baby. The neighbors, witnessing the commotion, offered their assistance, helping us gather our belongings and offering whatever support they could. It was a blur of activity, with bags and suitcases piled high as we were forced to leave our home.

As we stood outside, the reality of our predicament sunk in. It was sweltering hot, and we had nowhere to go. I had given birth just a few weeks prior, and now we were left homeless, with no plan and no resources to fall back on. It was a dire situation, and I felt a sense of panic creeping in.

In a stroke of luck, one of the neighbors offered us some money, a small gesture of kindness in our turmoil. With no other options, we decided to take the bus, riding aimlessly as we tried to figure out our next move. It was a desperate attempt to buy some time, to escape the suffocating heat and uncertainty that hung in the air.

As we rode the bus, I couldn't shake the feeling of despair that settled over me. My son's tiny body felt unnaturally warm, and I couldn't help but worry about his health. We were adrift, unsure of where to go or what to do next, our future uncertain and fraught with danger.

Eventually, we stumbled upon a place offering free food, a small reprieve from our hardship. But even as we ate, my mind was consumed with worry, the reality of our situation weighing heavily on my shoulders. We were alone, with no one to turn to and nowhere to call home.

As we continued to wander, my concerns for my son's health only grew. His feverish temperature persisted, and I worried that something serious might be wrong. Desperate to cool him down, I sought refuge in air-conditioned places like the mall and Walmart, hoping that the cooler environment would provide some relief for him.

Despite our dire circumstances, I was grateful for the support provided by programs like WIC, which ensured that we had access to essentials like baby formula and food. It was a small comfort amidst the chaos, but it helped alleviate some of the stress and worry of providing for my newborn son.

But even as we tried to navigate our new reality, tensions between Ty and me continued to simmer. His frustration and blame only added to my already heavy heart, as I grappled with the sudden upheaval of being kicked out by my own family. It was a betrayal that cut deep, leaving me feeling lost and alone in the world.

In a moment of desperation, we sought solace in a nearby church. While it wasn't my usual place of worship, I turned to prayer, seeking guidance and strength in our trials. As I poured out my heart to God, I prayed for a sign, a glimmer of hope to light our path forward in this dark and uncertain time.

As we settled into the hotel room, I couldn't shake the feeling of uncertainty that hung heavy in the air.

The temporary respite offered by the voucher was a welcome relief, but it was only a band-aid on the larger wound of our situation. With each passing day, the reality of our predicament loomed larger, casting a shadow over our fragile stability.

With limited resources at our disposal, I knew we needed to think outside the box to make ends meet. That's when I had the idea to leverage our food stamps to buy essential items from Walmart and resell them for a profit. It wasn't a perfect solution, but it was a temporary lifeline that helped us stay afloat a little while longer.

Ty took to the task with surprising enthusiasm, finding satisfaction in the small victories of each sale. His efforts put a few extra dollars in our pockets, enough to extend our stay at the hotel beyond the initial voucher period. But even as we celebrated these small wins, I couldn't shake the gnawing sense of urgency to find a more permanent solution.

As I sat in the hospital, grappling with the weight of our dire situation, a nurse took notice of my circumstances. She saw past the facade I was putting on, recognizing the signs of homelessness in the multiple suitcases by my side. With empathy in her eyes, she gently inquired about my well-being and offered a glimmer of hope in the form of Covenant House.

Covenant House—a beacon of support for young adults facing homelessness. It sounded like a lifeline, a chance for me to find some semblance of stability for myself and my baby. But as I considered this opportunity, the harsh reality set in Ty, my partner in this turbulent journey, wouldn't be able to accompany me. At 19, I was eligible for Covenant House, but Ty, older than me, didn't meet the criteria.

I faced a heart-wrenching dilemma—choose the shelter and security offered by Covenant House or remain on the streets with Ty, knowing that it meant sacrificing the chance for stability for myself and my baby. As I weighed my options, Ty's presence loomed large in my mind. Despite the strain in our relationship and the challenges we faced, I couldn't bear the thought of leaving him alone on the streets.

But as I shared the news with Ty, his reaction only added to the complexity of our predicament. He grappled with the reality of our situation, realizing that he wouldn't be able to join me at Covenant House. With uncertainty clouding his expression, he asked me what he was supposed to do—a question for which I had no easy answer.

As we stood outside the hospital, the weight of our circumstances pressing down upon us, my mother's voice echoed in the background, offering a glimmer of hope amidst the chaos. She reached out, expressing her desire to secure a low-income house for us, a gesture born out of guilt and a genuine desire to help. Yet, even as she extended this olive branch, I couldn't shake the resentment that simmered beneath the surface.

My mother's failure to stand up for us when we were kicked out of our family's home stung deeply, casting a shadow over our relationship. The lines between loyalty and self-preservation blurred as I grappled with conflicting emotions, torn between the desire for stability and the need to protect my sense of agency.

As I sat in the Greyhound station, clutching my baby and surrounded by suitcases filled with our meager belongings, a sense of uncertainty hung heavy in the air. The reality of my situation sunk in deeper with each passing moment, as I grappled with the weight of my decisions and the daunting journey that lay ahead.

Leaving Covenant House behind marked the end of one chapter and the beginning of another, one that was shrouded in uncertainty and filled with unanswered questions. With nowhere else to turn, I clung to the slim hope that returning to Miami might offer some semblance of stability, despite the fractured relationships and unresolved issues that awaited me there.

As I boarded the Greyhound bus bound for Miami, a mix of emotions swirled within me—fear, apprehension, and a glimmer of hope. The journey ahead loomed large and uncertain, yet I found solace in the presence of my baby, a constant reminder of the unwavering bond that anchored me amidst the storm.

The hours passed in a blur as the bus rumbled along the highway, each mile bringing me closer to the city I once called home. Memories of happier times mingled with the harsh realities of the present, casting a bittersweet shadow over my thoughts.

Arriving in Miami, I was greeted by the familiar sights and sounds of the city, yet it felt foreign and unfamiliar, tinged with the weight of my recent struggles. With no family to turn to and no clear path forward, I faced the daunting task of rebuilding my life from the ground up, armed only with the determination to create a better future for myself and my baby.

As I stood at the bus station, grappling with the weight of uncertainty and the burden of responsibility, a whirlwind of thoughts raced through my mind. The prospect of embarking on the journey alone with my baby seemed daunting, compounded by the uncertainty of what awaited me upon arrival in Miami.

Amidst the chaos of my thoughts, one question loomed large: should I reunite with Kevin, the potential father of my baby? The fractured nature of our relationship left me torn, unsure if imposing on his life was the right course of action.

As the bus pulled up to the station, reality set in—I had no money, no plan, and no clear path forward. The realization that I had been provided with only essentials for my baby, but not for myself, left me feeling utterly helpless and alone.

In a moment of clarity, I decided to forego boarding the bus, opting instead to confront the unknown and seek solace in the familiarity of home. With a heavy heart, I reached out to my mother, swallowing my pride and admitting defeat.

Upon returning home, the weight of the past two weeks lifted from my shoulders as my family enveloped me in their embrace. The simple act of holding my baby and being welcomed back into the warmth of my family brought a sense of relief and comfort that I hadn't realized I'd been yearning for.

Though the events that led me back home remained unspoken, the unspoken understanding and unwavering support of my family spoke volumes. As we shared a meal, the tensions of the past melted away, replaced by a sense of peace and gratitude for the safety and security of home.

Chapter 8:
The Unpaying (Pain) Guest

After a peaceful night's rest, I returned to my side of the house, where my family asked about Ty. Despite the hurtful things he had said and his lack of effort to provide for our baby, they expressed concern for his well-being. They even suggested that Ty could come back, but I was hesitant. Ty's behavior left me feeling angry and disappointed. He had options, like reaching out to his brother for help, but he refused. When my mom called Ty and invited him back, I could sense his reluctance. He returned, but his attitude was sour. He seemed resentful towards my mom and aunt, which only added to the tension in the house.

Ty's presence made things even more strained. He complained about being kicked out before and expressed distrust towards my family. His words only fueled my frustration. I didn't want to be caught in the middle of his conflicts with my mom and aunt. So, as time passed, my auntie Pam would often go to help another family member, leaving me to spend time next door talking to my mom. These conversations were a lifeline for me, a chance to share my thoughts and concerns. Meanwhile, Ty and I tried to rebuild our relationship, but it wasn't easy. We argued frequently, especially about money. Ty would spend his income recklessly on his own needs, neglecting his responsibilities as a father. I urged him to contribute to buying diapers for our baby, but it often fell on deaf ears.

Feeling the strain of our situation, I attempted to find work to ease our financial burden. I applied for a job at the Dollar Store but quickly realized that I couldn't juggle employment with the demands of caring for our child. I didn't have reliable childcare, and I didn't want to burden my mom with watching the baby while I worked.

As the pressure mounted, I found myself slipping into a deep depression. There were days when I felt like I was losing my grip on reality. I remember one particularly bad episode when I became overwhelmed with despair. I went to my mom and auntie Pam, pleading with them to let me handle things on my own and to consider asking Ty to leave. But they were hesitant, reluctant to repeat the cycle of kicking him out.

The tension in the air was palpable as Ty and I reached a breaking point. In a heated argument, I finally revealed to him about Kevin, the possibility that he might not be our baby's father. It was a desperate attempt to convey the depth of my frustration and dissatisfaction with our relationship. Ty's reaction was explosive. He advanced toward me aggressively, but my mom and Auntie Pam intervened, preventing the situation from escalating further.

As Ty processed the bombshell I had dropped, he became increasingly volatile. He threatened to harm himself, a pattern of behavior that had become all too familiar in our arguments. Although I initially took his threats seriously, I had grown numb to them over time. This time, however, my family managed to calm him down and persuade him to stay. I retreated with the baby, leaving them to handle the situation outside.

With Ty temporarily pacified, I found myself alone with my thoughts and the baby. It was a moment of respite amidst the chaos of our tumultuous relationship. Yet, deep down, I knew that our problems were far from resolved. As the days passed, I couldn't shake off the unease that lingered within me. The tension between Ty and me persisted, fluctuating between fleeting moments of calm and explosive arguments. Despite our differences, I couldn't deny the connection we shared during intimate moments, a bittersweet respite from our tumultuous reality.

Then, unexpectedly, life took another turn. I discovered I was pregnant again. The news hit me like a whirlwind, filling me with a mix of emotions ranging from shock to uncertainty. I confided in Ty about the pregnancy, hoping for reassurance or support, but instead, he expressed doubts and concerns. He suggested terminating the pregnancy, citing our precarious living situation and the challenges of raising another child.

His words pierced through me, leaving me feeling conflicted and alone. I grappled with the weight of his doubts and fears, questioning the future of our family and the stability of our relationship. Yet, amidst the turmoil, a glimmer of hope remained—the prospect of welcoming another life into this world, despite the uncertainties that lay ahead.

Despite Ty's reservations, I couldn't bring myself to consider terminating the pregnancy. I believed in the inherent value of life and held onto the possibility of a brighter future for our growing family. As time went on, I couldn't shake the feeling of being overwhelmed and stressed out. The weight of keeping the pregnancy a secret from my family began to take its toll. Ty's insistence on secrecy made me realize how much he controlled me over the years, dictating my actions and decisions. But I was determined to break free from his grasp.

When Auntie Pam wasn't around, I mustered the courage to confide in my mom about the pregnancy. Her joy and excitement were palpable, and she shared the news with the rest of the family. Despite the initial happiness, the atmosphere became strained when my niece and nephew visited. Their awkwardness mirrored the strained relationship I had with my sister.

On my birthday, June 9th, I woke up with a newfound sense of optimism. Pregnancy had brought unexpected changes to my appearance, clearing up my complexion and giving me a natural glow. It was the first time in a long while that I felt comfortable without makeup. Despite not having elaborate plans, I decided to make the most of the day. I visited my doctor's appointment and cherished the opportunity to bond with my baby.

While passing by my uncle's house, he greeted me with warm birthday wishes. My Uncle Anthony had always been a source of support, especially during challenging times. He expressed his concern for my well-being and shared in my joy on this special day. Despite the difficulties we faced, my family always made an effort to celebrate important occasions.

During the birthday celebration, my family mentioned JC, the person I considered to be like a father figure to me. I had spoken to him a few days prior, expressing my intention to celebrate Father's Day with him. Despite the distance, our bond remained strong, and I wanted to show my appreciation for his role in my life. Feelings of betrayal and hurt overwhelmed me as I grappled with the news of my father's passing. The weight of his absence bore down on me, leaving me unable to stand. My uncle, sensing my distress, offered comfort and support, urging me to stay with him. Clutching my swollen belly, tears streaming down my face, I felt a profound sense of loss.

When Ty arrived, oblivious to my anguish, I couldn't find solace in his presence. His indifference to my pain pierced through me, confirming my decision to part ways with him. My father's death marked a turning point in my life, awakening a desire for independence and self-reliance.

Despite my mother's attempts to shield me from distress, I confronted her about withholding the news. The realization that they had kept such a significant event from me only deepened my sense of isolation. As funeral arrangements were made, I struggled to find my place in the family dynamic, feeling sidelined and overlooked.

Amid the chaos surrounding my father's passing, the focus shifted to matters of inheritance and finances. I found myself embroiled in disputes over money, unable to properly grieve for my loss. My father, though not my biological parent, had always treated me and my sister as his own, regardless of DNA.

The tension escalated as family members debated who was entitled to what, overlooking the emotional toll of the situation. Frustration bubbled within me as discussions revolved solely around monetary concerns, disregarding the deeper significance of my father's legacy. In a moment of clarity, I lashed out, asserting that my priority was honoring my father's memory, not squabbling over material possessions.

During this tumultuous period, I encountered my Uncle Daisy's brother for the first time. Despite the somber circumstances, his presence offered a glimpse into my father's life beyond our immediate family. Yet, even in this moment of connection, the specter of greed loomed large, with insinuations that I was motivated by monetary gain.

However, amidst the turmoil, I remained steadfast in fulfilling my father's wishes. As I laid him to rest in 2014, heavily pregnant with my second child, I honored his memory by bestowing upon my daughter the name Christina—a nod to his enduring love and influence in my life. After the funeral, my feelings toward Ty changed drastically. His lack of support during such a difficult time made me realize that I couldn't rely on him. Even when I asked him to watch Tyrone for a few hours while I attended my father's funeral, he refused, leaving me feeling abandoned once again.

When I returned home and discussed my feelings with my mom, I expressed my desire to leave. I knew I needed to focus on being a mom to my two children, and I couldn't do that while living with Ty. My mom understood and supported my decision to find my place.

Together, my mom and I scoured the neighborhood for rental options, eventually finding an apartment for $900 a month. With my mom's financial assistance and my welfare benefits, I was able to afford the rent and bills on my own.

Moving into my place was a liberating experience. Although Ty expressed willingness to visit, I knew it was time to prioritize myself and my children. With my mom's help, I settled into my new home, and our relationship grew stronger as we bonded over preparations for the arrival of my daughter.

Moving out of that house with my mom brought us even closer together. We formed a strong bond, doing everything together. Whether it was going to doctor's appointments or simply spending time at home, we were inseparable.

One day, I woke up feeling intense pain in my stomach. My water broke, signaling that my second baby was on the way. I called Ty, but he didn't answer. My mom went next door to inform him, but he seemed paranoid about who would watch our son, Tyrone, while I went into labor.

Despite my reassurances, Ty insisted on staying behind with Tyrone. He promised to bring him to the hospital once the baby was born. I was disappointed by his paranoia, especially since my mom and Auntie Pam were more than capable of caring for Tyrone.

In the end, my mom accompanied me to the hospital, along with my grandma, who offered prayers and support. When I gave birth to my daughter, Maya Kushrina Holta, I had my mom, grandma, and Auntie Ursula by my side. Although Ty eventually visited the hospital to meet his daughter, I couldn't help but feel overwhelmed, especially as I thought about my dad not being there to witness the birth.

As I rested in the hospital, gazing at my newborn daughter, I couldn't shake the feeling of longing for my dad and the sadness of his absence. As time went on, my son was growing up quickly, while I adjusted to life with a newborn baby. It was undeniably overwhelming to have two young children to care for, but I managed. When the hospital released me a few days later and confirmed that Maya was healthy, I returned home to my new reality.

Moving out of my mom's house was a big step, but having her stay with me for a while helped ease the transition of caring for two babies. However, Ty seemed to have issues with my mom being around too much. He complained about not having alone time with me and voiced his frustrations, but I was fed up with his constant complaints. My focus was solely on being a mother and ensuring the well-being of my children.

Over time, I realized that I needed to assert my independence and learn how to navigate motherhood on my own. Despite my mom's continued visits, I started taking more responsibility for my kids without relying on her constant presence. This newfound independence also helped improve my relationship with Ty.

Although we still had arguments, particularly about financial matters, my mom's unwavering support and involvement brought us closer together. We began to enjoy simple activities together, like shopping at Walmart, making groceries, and taking walks. It was heartwarming to see my mom's joy whenever she spent time with her grandkids, and having her just down the street made it all the more special.

The incident with Auntie Pam left me shaken and filled with a mix of emotions. While I was grateful that Maya was unharmed, the thought of what could have happened haunted me. Auntie Pam's explanation that she might have saved Maya from a worse fate by breaking her fall didn't fully ease my anger and fear. It was a wake-up call for me as a parent, reminding me of the fragility of life and the need to be vigilant at all times.

In the aftermath of the incident, I found myself questioning who I could trust to care for my children.

The realization that accidents could happen even under the watch of a trusted family member made me hesitant to leave Maya or Tyrone with anyone else. I became hyper-aware of potential dangers around the house and took extra precautions to ensure their safety.

Despite my anger towards Auntie Pam, I couldn't ignore the possibility that it was indeed an accident. The guilt and remorse she expressed seemed genuine, and I grappled with conflicting emotions as I tried to make sense of what had happened. Deep down, I knew that harboring resentment would only weigh me down, so I tried to forgive Auntie Pam and move forward.

As time passed, Maya continued to thrive, and I became more confident in my ability to protect and care for her and Tyrone. The incident served as a reminder to cherish every moment with my children and to never take their safety for granted. While I couldn't erase the memory of that frightening day, I resolved to focus on creating a loving and nurturing environment for my family, where they could grow and flourish without fear.

Chapter 9:
A Mother's Struggle

As I reflect on my childhood, memories of my mother's battle with diabetes flood my mind. Her struggle was a constant presence in our lives. Unlike today, where there are numerous options and advancements in diabetes management, back then, it was a different story. I vividly remember watching her meticulously prick her finger to check her blood sugar levels, a routine that seemed to be a part of her daily life.

Her diabetes was a heavy burden, one that she carried with her every day. Despite her efforts, it was evident that she wasn't always able to manage it effectively. Her diet was often erratic, and she struggled to prioritize her health amidst the demands of daily life.

At this juncture in my life, my own family was growing. My son was just two years old, full of boundless energy and curiosity, while my daughter was a mere seven or eight months old. Amidst the chaos of parenthood, I found solace in the routine of caring for them, cherishing every moment spent together.

Despite the challenges my mother faced, she remained a pillar of strength for our family. Her resilience in the face of adversity taught me valuable lessons about perseverance and determination. Even during moments of uncertainty, she continued to prioritize our well-being above all else.

As I delved into the realm of co-parenting, life seemed to settle into a rhythm of its own. It was during this period that I crossed paths with Jimmy, just a week before my mother's passing. I remember the encounter vividly as if it were etched into my memory.

Struggling with the stroller outside, attempting to wrangle my children into it, I was met with unexpected assistance from Jimmy. His kind gesture of helping me with the stroller sparked the beginning of our acquaintance. He remarked on my youthful appearance, jokingly suggesting that I looked much younger than my actual age of 22 at the time.

Despite his light-hearted banter, there was a sincerity in his demeanor that intrigued me. Our conversation flowed effortlessly as he shared that he frequented the area to visit his aunt, who happened to live nearby. It was apparent that there was a genuine interest in getting to know me better, as he requested my phone number before parting ways.

True to his word, Jimmy reached out a couple of days later, expressing his desire to drop by and chat while he was in the neighborhood visiting his aunt. I welcomed the idea, intrigued by the prospect of getting to know him better outside of our initial encounter.

When Jimmy arrived, he introduced me to his aunt, whom I recognized from the neighborhood. Their warmth and familiarity put me at ease as we engaged in conversation. Jimmy's curiosity about my life, particularly regarding the children's father, led to a discussion about co-parenting and the dynamics of my situation.

I appreciated his nonjudgmental approach and his willingness to accept me for who I was. Our interaction gradually evolved from acquaintances to friends, as we navigated the complexities of our respective lives together.

As Jimmy and I continued to nurture our friendship, our interactions deepened through conversations and texts. I found comfort in confiding in him about my life, including the dynamics of my relationship with Ty and the challenges of co-parenting.

Sharing the news of my newfound friendship with Jimmy with my mother, she expressed her support and encouragement, reminding me of the importance of fostering meaningful connections in my life. Despite the complexities of my relationship with Ty, I reassured her that Jimmy was simply a friend, nothing more.

However, the transition from acquaintances to friends took an unexpected turn when Ty encountered Jimmy for the first time. His reaction was one of suspicion and hostility, his protective instincts kicking into overdrive as he questioned Jimmy's presence near our home.

Attempting to diffuse the tension, I introduced Ty to Jimmy, hoping to ease his concerns. But Ty's apprehension only escalated, demanding Jimmy leave and expressing his disapproval of his presence around our children.

Feeling caught in the middle, I urged Jimmy to depart, opting to address Ty's concerns privately. In a heartfelt conversation, I reiterated that while Jimmy was indeed a friend, our romantic relationship was long over, and we were now focused solely on co-parenting.

Ty's reaction was one of disbelief and hurt, unaware that our relationship had reached its conclusion. As I stood my ground, explaining to Ty that my decision to leave the house was not to escape my mother, but rather to distance myself from him and the chaos he brought into our lives, I hoped he would understand. Our relationship had long ceased to be romantic, existing solely as co-parents focused on our children's well-being.

However, Ty's inability to grasp the finality of our relationship led to further conflict and his eventual disappearance from our lives. His absence created a void, especially for our son, who looked forward to visiting his grandmother next door whenever he went to see his father. My mother, always welcoming, would eagerly prepare meals for them, bridging the gap left by Ty's departure.

During this upheaval, I found solace in conversations with my mother, who became my confidante during those tumultuous times. Little did I know that our last conversation on July 24th would be our final exchange.

As she expressed her love for me and the children, bidding us goodnight, I never imagined it would be the last time I heard her voice. The following morning, as my phone incessantly rang, I assumed it was my mother calling as she often did in the early hours. Engrossed in my morning routine, I brushed off the calls, assuming she was occupied elsewhere.

But as the calls persisted and my son, barely two years old at the time, eagerly tried to answer the phone, a sense of unease began to creep in. Little did I know, those persistent calls were not from my mother but rather the harbinger of a tragedy that would forever alter the course of our lives.

As I finally glanced at my phone, the sheer number of missed calls from my Auntie Pam and Aunt Ursula sent a shiver down my spine. Before I could even contemplate returning their calls, the phone rang once more, this time with Auntie Ursula delivering the devastating news – my mother was not breathing, and she was being rushed to the hospital.

Panic set in as my hands trembled at the gravity of the situation. Questions raced through my mind as I struggled to comprehend the reality of what I had just been told. With Ty already en route to my house, I knew I had to act quickly. Leaving the kids inside, I dashed out, my heart pounding with fear and uncertainty.

The sweltering summer heat bore down on me as I ran, the weight of the situation heavy on my shoulders. Neighbors gathered outside, their concerned voices blending into a cacophony of worry as they inquired about my mother's well-being. Amidst the chaos, I could only offer a helpless shrug, my mind consumed by the urgency of reaching my mother's side.

Arriving at her house, the sight of my family gathered outside only intensified my apprehension. Pushing through the crowd, I hurried inside, my eyes scanning the room until they landed on the harrowing scene before me – my mother lying motionless on the floor, paramedics attending to her in a frantic bid to revive her.

As the paramedics tirelessly performed CPR on my mother, the gravity of the situation weighed heavily on everyone gathered outside. My sister, cousins, aunties, uncles, and even my grandmother stood vigil, their anxious faces mirroring the turmoil within me. Inside, I stood alone, helplessly watching as they continued their efforts, clinging to the hope that she would pull through.

Amidst the chaos, the words "time of death, noon." pierced through the air, shattering any semblance of hope I held onto. Collapsing to the floor, my world crumbled around me as the reality of my mother's passing sank in. Tears flowed freely as I grappled with the enormity of my loss, surrounded by the anguish of my family outside.

Amid my grief, I knew I had to inform Ty of the devastating news. His somber acceptance mirrored my own, as we navigated the painful reality of our loss together. With my Auntie Pam's guidance, we made the difficult decision to bring the children to my mother's house, where we waited for hours, enveloped in a surreal haze of sorrow and disbelief.

As I watched my children playing on the floor, my daughter crawling while my son was lost in his toys, the reality of my mother's sudden absence hit me like a tidal wave. She had been the anchor in their lives, the one who showered them with love and attention, and now, with her gone, I couldn't help but worry about the difficult moments they would face without her guidance.

Hours seemed to stretch into eternity as we waited for the authorities to arrive and take my mother's body. Amidst the somber atmosphere, a fleeting thought of my mother's love for chicken crossed my mind, a small detail amidst the overwhelming grief. But when we ventured to my grandmother's house, hoping for some semblance of solace, we found it empty, the absence of family leaving us feeling adrift.

After my mother's passing, Jimmy's presence provided a semblance of support amidst the overwhelming grief. When he arrived at my house and learned of the situation, his reaction was one of genuine concern and empathy. Sensing my need for space, he took charge of caring for the children before quietly departing, leaving me to grapple with the weight of my loss.

As the days passed and funeral arrangements were made, I found myself submerged in a fog of sorrow, allowing my family to handle the necessary preparations. In honoring my mother's memory, I ensured that she was laid to rest in her favorite color, a fitting tribute to her vibrant spirit.

Meanwhile, Jimmy's actions spoke volumes about his character, as he rallied support from the entire neighborhood, spreading the word of my mother's passing and inviting others to offer their condolences. Even his ex-girlfriend, who had her reservations about him, extended her sympathies, albeit with a cautionary warning about his past behavior.

Caught amid grief and vulnerability, I brushed aside her concerns, attributing them to jealousy or bitterness over our budding friendship. Confronted with her words, I broached the topic with Jimmy, seeking reassurance about his intentions and character. His response was dismissive, brushing off her claims and affirming our platonic relationship.

As the day of the funeral arrived, tensions with Ty reached a boiling point as he made the solemn occasion even more challenging. Amidst the chaos of saying goodbye to my mother, I found myself juggling the responsibilities of parenthood, struggling to manage both my grief and the needs of my young children.

Despite my efforts to navigate the emotional turmoil, Ty's presence only added to the chaos. His reluctance to cooperate, coupled with his disdain for Jimmy's support, further strained our already fraught relationship. It was a heartbreaking moment as I watched him leave with the children, leaving me to grapple with my grief alone.

Desperate for a moment of respite, I made the difficult decision to entrust my children to my mother's care, seeking solace in the familiarity of her home. With the funeral hall conveniently located nearby, I knew they would be safe under her watchful eye as I faced the painful task of bidding farewell to my beloved mother.

Returning from the funeral, I found myself grappling with a mix of emotions, seeking solace in the familiar presence of Jimmy. Yet, our interaction quickly turned into a confrontation as I confronted him about his behavior. It was evident that Ty's animosity towards him stemmed from his insecurities, projecting his fears onto me and our children.

Despite his own experiences with co-parenting, Jimmy remained a source of support and understanding, offering insights gleaned from his journey as a father. His genuine concern for my well-being and that of my family was evident, even as he navigated the complexities of our evolving relationship.

As we shared a meal, Jimmy's attention turned to my sister, offering a compliment that briefly lifted the heaviness of the moment. His words served as a reminder of the beauty and strength of my family, despite the challenges we faced.

But as the evening drew to a close, I found myself needing space to process the events of the day. Politely declining Jimmy's advances, I retreated into solitude, craving a moment of solitude to reflect and mourn in peace.

In the days that followed, my relationship with Jimmy deepened, and I found myself grappling with his increasing distance and the sudden shift in his priorities. Despite initially seeking solace in his presence, his frequent visits became tinged with a sense of obligation, his requests for money leaving me feeling used and unappreciated.

Caught in the throes of grief and desperation, I turned to weed as a coping mechanism, seeking refuge in its numbing embrace to dull the pain of my loss. Each hit offered temporary respite from the overwhelming weight of my emotions, allowing me to escape the harsh realities of my situation, if only for a moment.

Yet, as the days stretched into weeks, the isolation and abandonment I felt only deepened. Bereft of support from my family, I found myself sinking deeper into a cycle of dependency, the haze of drugs offering fleeting moments of relief from the crushing loneliness that engulfed me.

Lost in a fog of despair, I retreated further into myself, the walls of my home becoming both sanctuary and prison. Days blurred into nights as I grappled with the void left by my mother's passing, seeking solace in the only comfort I knew – the numbing embrace of intoxication.

Lost in a haze of addiction and despair, I found myself trapped in a downward spiral, unable to break free from the grip of substance abuse. As my dependence on weed grew, so too did Jimmy's demands for money, his requests becoming increasingly frequent and exorbitant.

Despite my initial willingness to provide for him, I soon began to feel the weight of his expectations bearing down on me, the realization dawning that I was being taken advantage of for his gain. Yet, mired in my turmoil, I lacked the clarity and strength to extricate myself from his grasp.

Amidst this tumultuous backdrop, the boundaries between us blurred, our interactions transitioning from platonic to something more intimate. Yet, even as I sought solace in his embrace, I couldn't shake the feeling that I was merely a pawn in his game, a means to an end in his pursuit of gratification and financial gain.

Caught in a web of dependency and manipulation, I struggled to reclaim agency over my life, my sense of self eroded by the toxic dynamic that had come to define our relationship. As I grappled with the consequences of Jimmy's betrayal, I found myself confronting the harsh reality of my situation. The news of the STD he had transmitted to me shook me to my core, forcing me to confront the reckless disregard he had shown for my well-being.

Though I couldn't fault him for his actions, as our relationship had never been defined by exclusivity, the sense of betrayal and violation I felt was undeniable. It was a stark reminder of the risks I had unwittingly exposed myself to in my quest for solace amidst the turmoil of my grief.

Yet, even as I wrestled with the fallout from Jimmy's revelation, another reckoning loomed on the horizon. With my mother's passing, the dynamics of my living situation had shifted, prompting me to make the difficult decision to vacate the rental property I had called home.

As I settled into my new life in my mother's house, the transition wasn't without its challenges.

Convincing Ty to vacate the premises proved to be a drawn-out ordeal, but eventually, he found alternative accommodation nearby, easing the tension between us. He remained a presence in our lives, visiting the kids regularly and even securing a job at a nearby store.

Meanwhile, my relationship with Jimmy continued to evolve, albeit with its own set of complications. Despite the conflicts that arose whenever he and Ty crossed paths, I found myself drawn further into Jimmy's orbit, eventually entering into a committed relationship with him.

With Jimmy's support, I embarked on this journey of self-improvement, attending classes and striving to carve out a better future for myself and my family. Yet, even as I pursued my educational goals, the specter of addiction continued to haunt me, casting a shadow over my efforts to move forward.

The weed, once a source of temporary relief from my pain, now served as a barrier to my progress, clouding my judgment and hindering my ability to fulfill my responsibilities as a mother. Despite my best intentions, I found myself trapped in a cycle of dependency, unable to break free from its grasp.

As the months passed and my children grew older, I grappled with the conflicting demands of motherhood and addiction, each day a battle against the debilitating effects of substance abuse. Yet, even in the depths of despair, a glimmer of hope remained, a flicker of resilience that refused to be extinguished.

Chapter 10:
Overcoming Challenges

As I struggled with addiction, I found myself in a constant battle between the numbing effects of substance abuse and the responsibilities of motherhood. Each day was a delicate balancing act, as I sought refuge in drugs to alleviate the pain that seemed insurmountable.

The allure of being high provided a temporary escape from the harsh realities of life, but it came at a steep cost. There were moments when I was so lost in my haze that I put my children's safety at risk, like the time I nearly caused a fire by forgetting about food in the oven.

Despite the dangers and consequences, the temporary relief offered by drugs seemed preferable to the unrelenting agony I experienced when sober. The cycle of addiction became a vicious trap, leaving me feeling trapped and powerless.

Even as I pursued my GED and attended classes, the grip of addiction threatened to derail my progress. There were days when I struggled to focus, my mind clouded by the effects of substance abuse, but I knew that I had to persevere for the sake of my children's future.

Opening up to my teacher about my struggles as a single mother and my history with special education was a daunting but necessary step. Fortunately, she proved to be understanding and supportive, offering me the encouragement and guidance I needed to succeed.

Despite my limited educational background, I was determined to overcome my challenges. While my knowledge of mathematics was rudimentary at best, I was willing to put in the effort to learn and improve, even if it meant starting from the basics like times tables.

With the support of my teacher and my determination, I began to make progress in my studies. Each small victory bolstered my confidence and reminded me that I was capable of achieving more than I ever thought possible.

As I struggled to grasp the concepts required for my GED, especially in math, I found myself hitting a roadblock. Despite my teacher's unwavering dedication and patience, I couldn't seem to overcome my mental barriers. The pressure to pass the math portion of the GED exam loomed over me, threatening to derail my progress.

Feeling overwhelmed and discouraged, I made the difficult decision to take a break from my studies. During this time, Ty, my children's father, faced challenges as he struggled with housing instability and conflicts with his living arrangements. Despite our complicated history, I couldn't turn him away when he needed a place to stay.

However, what started as a gesture of compassion quickly turned into a nightmare. Tensions escalated one evening when Jimmy, my current partner, came to visit. Ty's presence in the house, which he had initially agreed to, suddenly became a source of contention. A heated confrontation ensued, leading to a violent altercation that left both Jimmy and Ty injured.

In the chaos of the moment, I frantically called the police, hoping to diffuse the situation before it escalated further. As they arrived on the scene, Jimmy was taken into custody, and I was left grappling with the aftermath of the violence that had erupted in my own home.

After the tumultuous incident with Ty and Jimmy, I found myself reevaluating my relationships and priorities. While Ty was taken into custody by the police the following day, Jimmy chose not to press charges, considering the impact on our children. However, the strain on our relationship was palpable, and I began to question whether Jimmy was truly committed to being a positive influence in our lives.

Despite the challenges, I resolved to focus on my education and enrolled back in GED classes. With my children in daycare, I could dedicate more time to my studies. Additionally, I decided to move next door to my Auntie Pam, who graciously offered me a place to stay.

As Ty settled into his new living arrangement, tensions between him and Jimmy simmered down. However, Jimmy's visits became less frequent, and our communication dwindled. I couldn't shake the memory of our first violent encounter, which had left me shaken and uncertain about our future together.

Jimmy's apologies and promises of change seemed convincing, especially when he invoked the memory of my late mother, exploiting my vulnerability in the process. Each time we neared a breakup, he would manipulate me into staying, using my grief as leverage.

As we continued our relationship, Jimmy introduced me to his older son, who eyed me suspiciously. It was clear that our dynamic was becoming increasingly strained, with tensions simmering just beneath the surface. Despite the warning signs, I chose to forgive Jimmy once again and allowed him back into my life.

However, the peace was short-lived. One rainy day, Jimmy's anger flared up again. He pounded on the door until he found his way inside, where he unleashed his fury on me, leaving me bruised and battered. It was a harrowing experience that left me shaken to my core.

Despite my efforts to maintain a semblance of normalcy in our relationship, I couldn't shake the feeling that Jimmy was keeping me hidden, perhaps ashamed of our connection. While he had a vehicle, he rarely took me anywhere or introduced me to his social circle. Nevertheless, I remained committed to my goals, including obtaining my GED.

After several years of perseverance, I finally achieved my goal of earning my GED. It was a significant milestone for me, representing a triumph over adversity and a step towards a brighter future. Although my achievement wasn't celebrated with fanfare-like others, it held immense personal significance.

After earning my GED, I took some time off to reflect on my next steps. During this period, I found solace in getting high, using it as a coping mechanism to numb the pain and uncertainty in my life. However, things took a darker turn when Jimmy's abusive behavior escalated.

Despite my efforts to include Jimmy in my family life by introducing him to my grandmother and sharing moments with my kids, his abusive tendencies persisted. Meanwhile, I turned to social media as an outlet to express my struggles, sharing my journey as a grieving single mother navigating co-parenting with my baby daddy, who lived nearby.

As I shared my experiences online, I received messages of support from acquaintances and strangers alike, offering words of encouragement and empathy. However, little did I know that this newfound exposure would lead to unforeseen consequences in my already tumultuous life.

That terrifying night, Jimmy's jealousy and possessiveness reached a dangerous peak. He discovered messages from Amir on my phone and erupted into a violent rage, accusing me of betrayal. In the dead of night, he mercilessly beat me, inflicting injuries on me and even harming my beloved dog. The sight of my sister receiving affectionate messages from him added to my pain, highlighting his hypocrisy and cruelty.

As the situation escalated, Jimmy retrieved a knife from the kitchen, sending shivers of fear down my spine. In a desperate bid to protect my children and myself, I fled outside with my daughter, while my son sought refuge under the bed, terrified. It was the early hours of the morning, and as I trembled outside with my child, a kind stranger appeared, offering assistance and ensuring our safety. Their timely intervention prevented a tragedy and compelled Jimmy to leave, albeit reluctantly.

Despite my strides in education and career aspirations, my self-esteem remained fragile, tethering me to unhealthy relationships. Jimmy, despite his violent outbursts, was a constant presence in my life. As I completed my GED and pursued a nursing program, the demands of balancing motherhood and education weighed heavily on me. When the nursing program proved too demanding, I shifted gears to hospitality, finding solace in the prospect of a career where I could help others.

As Jimmy's true nature began to reveal itself, I found myself increasingly disillusioned with our relationship. His supposed employment at a barbershop turned out to be a facade, with him resorting to sporadic house calls to make ends meet. His desire to become a tattoo artist led me to purchase a tattoo gun for him, only for it to gather dust as he failed to capitalize on the opportunity. Money became a constant source of tension between us, with his reliance on me for financial support becoming increasingly burdensome.

During that tumultuous time when Jimmy was incarcerated, my world seemed to spiral further out of control. Desperate to secure his release, I exhausted every avenue available to me, even as I grappled with my feelings of worthlessness. Despite my efforts, I found myself unable to bail him out, a stark reminder of my limitations and the depths of his legal troubles.

As I navigated through this ordeal, Jimmy's son emerged as an unexpected source of solace and connection. In moments of vulnerability, he confided in me, sharing intimate details of his upbringing and the strained relationship he shared with his father. It was in one of these vulnerable moments that our relationship took an unexpected turn, culminating in a regrettable act of intimacy that left me grappling with guilt and remorse.

When I mustered the courage to confess my indiscretion to Jimmy, the repercussions were swift and painful. His betrayal cut me deeply, plunging me into a whirlwind of conflicting emotions and self-recrimination. Amidst the chaos of Jimmy's incarceration, I found myself confronting the harsh reality of my choices and the consequences they wrought upon us all.

While grappling with the fallout of my actions and Jimmy's incarceration, another devastating blow struck our family. My beloved grandmother, the cornerstone of our family, was diagnosed with cancer. Learning of her diagnosis shattered me, plunging me into a whirlwind of emotions as I struggled to come to terms with the gravity of the situation.

Despite the weight of my challenges, I knew I needed to be there for my grandmother in her time of need. Rushing to her side, I held her hand tightly, my heart heavy with regret for not being more present in her life. Tears streamed down my face as I confessed my shortcomings, but my grandmother's response was one of unwavering love and understanding.

With compassion in her eyes, she reassured me that she knew the struggles I faced, even when I thought I was hiding them well. Her words cut through the haze of my pain, urging me to confront the reality of my situation and find the strength to chart a new path forward. In that moment, her wisdom became a beacon of hope, guiding me toward a future filled with purpose and determination.

My grandmother's words echoed in my mind, serving as a guiding light through the darkness that clouded my thoughts. She encouraged me to press on, reminding me of my resilience and capacity to overcome obstacles. With her unwavering support, I found renewed determination to see my journey through.

As I juggled the demands of my studies and the weight of my grandmother's illness, I made it a priority to spend as much time with her as possible. Each visit became a cherished moment, filled with bittersweet memories and the undeniable bond between us. Despite the toll that her illness had taken on her appearance, my grandmother's love remained a steadfast beacon of strength for me and my children.

Though my daughter struggled to understand the changes she saw in her beloved grandmother, I held her close, reassuring her that love transcended appearances. Together, we navigated the complexities of grief and uncertainty, finding solace in each other's presence and the enduring legacy of love that my grandmother had instilled within us.

As the days passed and my grandmother's condition worsened, I grappled with the inevitable loss that loomed on the horizon. Yet, amidst the pain and sorrow, I clung to the lessons she had imparted to me, drawing strength from her wisdom and the unbreakable bond we shared. And though the journey ahead was fraught with challenges, I vowed to honor her memory by forging ahead with courage and resilience, determined to build a brighter future for myself and my children.

In addition to quitting weed, I sought professional help through counseling. Opening up about my experiences with Kevin, Ty, and Jimmy was challenging, but it was a necessary step towards healing. Each counseling session provided me with a safe space to unpack my emotions and receive valuable guidance on how to navigate the complexities of my past.

Meanwhile, my Auntie Pam's presence next door brought a sense of comfort and stability to our lives. The kids enjoyed the newfound freedom of running between our houses, creating joyful memories amidst the turmoil of our circumstances. With Auntie Pam's support and the love of my children, I found the strength to confront my past and embrace the journey towards a brighter future.

With Jimmy out of my life, I finally felt a sense of relief. I had mustered the courage to end our toxic relationship, and I knew it was the right decision for me and my children. When Jimmy showed up at my door after his release from jail, I stood my ground and firmly told him that our relationship was over. I made it clear that he wasn't welcome in my life anymore and that I needed to prioritize the well-being of myself and my kids.

Just two weeks later, tragedy struck again. I received a devastating call from my auntie Pam, who was in tears as she informed me that my beloved grandma had passed away. I rushed to her house, leaving my son at home and taking my daughter with me. When we arrived, I witnessed the frantic efforts of paramedics trying to revive my grandma. It was a heartbreaking scene, and my daughter's tears only added to the sorrow permeating the air.

Despite my auntie's suggestion to shield my daughter from the trauma, I felt it was important for her to understand the reality of life and death. As we stood by my grandma's side, I couldn't help but reflect on the profound impact she had on my life and the invaluable lessons she had imparted to me.

Amid my grief, I couldn't shake the realization that cancer had claimed yet another precious soul in my family. The pain of losing my grandma only intensified the emotional turmoil I had been grappling with for so long. But amidst the sorrow, I found solace in the memories of her strength, wisdom, and unwavering love.

After my grandma's passing, I felt completely adrift. Her absence left a void in my life that I didn't know how to fill. I mourned her loss for weeks, shedding tears day and night as I grappled with the reality of her absence. She had always been a beacon of strength and resilience, so her sudden departure from this world felt like a cruel twist of fate.

Amid my grief, I found some semblance of comfort in the memories of our time together and the wisdom she had imparted to me. But I also couldn't shake the feeling of regret for not spending more time with her, for not being there for her when she needed me the most. It was a painful realization that haunted me in the days following her passing.

Despite my emotional turmoil, I knew I had to be strong for my children, especially as we navigated through the funeral proceedings and the aftermath of our loss. Jimmy, to his credit, managed to keep it together during the funeral, showing a level of maturity and restraint that I hadn't seen before. He seemed to understand the gravity of the situation and made an effort to support me and the kids during this difficult time.

However, as the weeks passed and the initial shock of my grandma's death began to wear off, Jimmy's behavior started to regress. Old patterns resurfaced, and I found myself once again grappling with his unpredictable and sometimes volatile demeanor. It was a stark reminder that while I had managed to extricate myself from one toxic relationship, the journey toward healing and self-discovery was far from over.

Chapter 11:
Facing Shadows

After my grandma passed away, it felt like a piece of my heart was missing. But I knew she wouldn't want me to give up on my dreams. So, even though I was hurting, I kept pushing forward. I went back to my classes, determined to finish what I started.

By this time, Jimmy was out of my life for good. I made sure of that. Ty was living next door, and we were doing our best to co-parent our kids. It wasn't easy, but we were making it work.

But the grief was still there, weighing me down like a heavy blanket. Sometimes, it felt like I couldn't breathe, like the pain was suffocating me. And in those moments, I turned to my old coping mechanisms.

I slowed down on the drugs, trying to use them less as a crutch. But sometimes, the pain was just too much to bear. So, I started sleeping around, trying to numb the ache inside me with fleeting moments of pleasure.

I'd wait at the bus stop, and guys would pull up, honking their horns and calling out to me. It was dangerous, but I didn't care. I just wanted to feel something other than the pain.

I'd get in the car with these guys, not knowing their names or anything about them. They'd offer to take me to class, but they always wanted something in return. And I... I'd give it to them, right there in the backseat of their cars.

Looking back, I realize how dangerous it was. I was putting myself at risk, both physically and emotionally. But in those moments, I didn't care. I just wanted to escape, even if it was just for a little while.

I did this with maybe four or five guys, I'm not proud to admit. It didn't mean anything to me, and it certainly didn't turn into anything more than a one-time thing. I didn't even know their names, and they didn't know mine. It was just... just sleeping around.

But one day, it all came crashing down. I was waiting for the bus, not even going to class this time.

And this guy pulled up, asking if I wanted a ride. I said yes, not thinking anything of it.

He drove me to where I needed to go, but then he said he wanted to take me to his place. I was standing outside the building, unsure of what to do. The guy was insisting that I come with him to his house, but I was hesitant. I knew I had to get back home to my kids, but he kept pushing, saying it would be fine.

He waited in the parking lot while I went inside to sign some papers. Everything seemed normal until the lady helping me asked if I had a ride. I told her about the guy waiting in the car, and that's when things took a scary turn.

The lady recognized the guy's car and warned me not to get in with him. She told me about another woman who had disappeared after getting into his car. She said he was dangerous, and I should stay away from him.

I was shaken, but I didn't know what to do. Then, the guy got out of the car and started insisting that I come with him. The lady and I hurried back inside the building and called the police.

When the police arrived, they asked me if I knew the guy. I told them I had just met him and got into his car. They told me how dangerous that was and went to talk to the guy.

He was adamant that I go with him, but the police intervened and made him leave. They gave me a ride home, and as I sat in the backseat, all I could think about was how close I had come to danger.

It was a wake-up call for me. I realized that what I was doing was incredibly risky. I could have lost my life that day, all because I was trying to numb the pain I was feeling inside.

After that scary encounter, I felt ashamed of myself. That wasn't the person I knew myself to be. I'd never put myself in risky situations like that before. Waiting for the bus was just a part of my routine, and I'd always been patient, no matter how long it took.

So, realizing that I'd gotten into a stranger's car, not once, but multiple times, was a wake-up call. I couldn't believe I had put myself in such danger. I didn't tell anyone about it, not even my guardian angel. I just stopped doing it altogether.

The lady who warned me about the guy reached out to make sure I got home safely. Her kindness meant a lot to me. I truly believe she saved my life that day. Who knows what could have happened if she hadn't intervened.

After that incident, things between Ty and me started to get tense. Living next door to each other meant he felt entitled to come over whenever he wanted. We argued a lot about the kids—how to discipline them, when to give them treats, things like that.

It was tough because we both wanted what was best for them, but we had different ideas about how to achieve that. Our arguments became more frequent, and tensions were running high.

Despite our disagreements, Ty and I were still trying to co-parent as best as we could. We both loved our kids and wanted to do right by them, but finding common ground was proving to be a challenge.

On top of all that, I was still dealing with the grief of losing my grandma. Her absence left a void in my life that I didn't know how to fill. I missed her wisdom, her laughter, her love. It felt like a piece of me was missing without her.

But I knew I had to keep pushing forward, for myself and for my kids. I threw myself into my studies and work, trying to distract myself from the pain. It wasn't easy, but I was determined to keep moving forward.

As time went on, I started to feel a sense of hope again. I knew that healing would take time, but I was making progress. And with each passing day, I grew stronger and more resilient.

One day in the middle of the night, with me in severe pain and my Aunt Pam taking charge. He insisted that Lakeside Hospital was the best option even though it was far away. I trusted his judgment, hoping that maybe this time, we would finally get some answers and relief.

As we rushed to Lakeside Hospital, I couldn't help but feel scared and anxious. The pain in my back and stomach was relentless, and I just wanted it to stop. Ty was by my side, trying to comfort me as best as he could, but I could tell he was worried too.

When we arrived at Lakeside Hospital, the medical staff sprang into action. So there I was, rushed into the hospital with my auntie Pam and Ty by my side. The medical team at Lakeside Hospital wasted no time. They whisked me away for X-rays and other tests to figure out what was causing my unbearable pain.

I remember being placed in a machine, unable to stand straight because of the agony coursing through my body. But those tests revealed something alarming – there was a serious issue with my liver that required immediate attention.

The doctor didn't mince words. He told me that if I hadn't come to the hospital when I did, I could have lost my life within 24 hours. It was a sobering realization that sent shivers down my spine. I was grateful beyond words that fate had led me to Lakeside Hospital.

Without hesitation, the medical team prepared me for surgery. Everything moved at lightning speed, and before I knew it, I was being wheeled into the operating room. As they put me under anesthesia, I couldn't help but wonder how close I had come to the brink of death without even realizing it.

When I woke up after the surgery, surrounded by my loved ones, I felt an overwhelming sense of relief. My family's presence gave me strength and hope during those dark moments. I couldn't have asked for a more supportive group by my side.

Recovery was slow and painful. I spent a week in the hospital, unable to move around freely. Even after I was discharged, walking was a challenge, and I had to take time off from my classes to focus on healing.

As I lay in my hospital bed, reflecting on the events that led me here, I couldn't help but feel a mix of emotions. I was grateful to be alive, but I also felt anger and frustration towards Tulane Hospital for neglecting to properly diagnose my condition earlier.

When I questioned the doctors about why Tulane hadn't caught the issue sooner, their response was infuriating. They admitted that they hadn't conducted the necessary tests, unlike Lakeside Hospital, which sprang into action as soon as I arrived.

My auntie Pam was livid, and rightfully so. She had been tirelessly advocating for my health, only to be met with indifference and negligence from the medical professionals at Tulane. It was a wake-up call for all of us about the importance of being proactive about our health and seeking second opinions when necessary.

As I continued to heal, tensions between Ty and my auntie Pam simmered beneath the surface. Ty had his way of handling things with the kids, and my auntie Pam had hers. Their conflicting styles led to frequent disagreements, leaving me caught in the middle.

My auntie Pam, feeling overwhelmed by the constant friction, decided to spend more time at my late grandma's house. It was her way of seeking solace and a break from the tension at home. She assured me that she was just a phone call away if I needed anything, but her absence left a noticeable void in our household.

With my auntie Pam gone more often, the weight of responsibility fell squarely on my shoulders. I found myself juggling household chores, caring for the kids, and trying to maintain some sense of normalcy amidst the chaos. Meanwhile, Ty's involvement seemed to dwindle, adding to the strain in our relationship.

Our arguments became more frequent as resentment brewed between us. I felt overwhelmed and exhausted, grappling with the demands of motherhood and my own health struggles. Despite my best efforts to keep the peace, tensions continued to escalate, pushing us further apart.

Eventually, as I regained my strength and was able to return to my classes, I found solace in my studies. Pursuing my hospitality certificate provided a welcome distraction from the turmoil at home. I threw myself into my coursework, relishing the opportunity to focus on something other than the challenges of daily life.

But just as I was beginning to find my footing again, another blow struck. My once-luscious hair, a source of pride and confidence, began to fall out. It was a devastating blow to my self-esteem, shattering the image I had of myself as a strong, resilient woman.

For many black women like me, our hair is more than just a physical attribute – it's a symbol of beauty, identity, and cultural heritage. To see my hair thinning and falling out felt like losing a part of myself, leaving me feeling vulnerable and insecure.

Losing my hair was a devastating blow, one that I struggled to come to terms with. I blamed the stress and the tight braids for causing my hair to thin and fall out in clumps. The sight of my once-voluminous locks dwindling to almost nothing was heart-wrenching, and I knew I had to find a solution.

Feeling self-conscious and insecure, I turned to wigs as a temporary fix. It wasn't easy, though. Wearing wigs made me feel like I was hiding behind a mask, concealing my true self beneath layers of synthetic hair. But I didn't have much of a choice – I couldn't bear the thought of being seen without my hair.

Despite my efforts to maintain a sense of normalcy, tensions with Ty continued to escalate. One particularly heated argument stands out in my memory – Ty unleashed a barrage of hurtful words, belittling me in front of our neighbors. He accused me of being dumb, of dropping out of school, and of making poor choices in life.

His words cut deep, reopening old wounds and stirring up feelings of inadequacy and shame. I couldn't believe that he would use my past struggles against me, throwing them in my face as if they were weapons. The pain of his betrayal was almost too much to bear.

In a moment of anger and frustration, I lashed out, hurling insults back at him in a futile attempt to defend myself. But deep down, I knew that his words had already struck a chord, leaving me feeling wounded and vulnerable.

As our argument escalated, the neighbors looked on, their curious eyes adding to the humiliation I felt. I wanted nothing more than to escape, to retreat into the safety of my own home and lick my wounds in private. But there was no escaping the harsh reality of our crumbling relationship, no matter how hard I tried to deny it.

Chapter 12:
Overcoming Obstacles and Embracing New Beginnings

Watching the fear in my kids' eyes as Ty's anger erupted into violence was heartbreaking. They began to cower and retreat whenever he entered the house, his presence casting a shadow of dread over our home. One particularly alarming incident stands out in my memory – the day Ty punched a hole in the wall, sending the kids into a frenzy of tears and screams. As he lashed out in anger, I knew something had to change.

Despite my efforts to shield them from the toxicity of our relationship, Ty began to poison their minds against me, filling their impressionable young minds with hurtful lies and accusations. It was then that I knew I had to put an end to the chaos, for the sake of my children's well-being.

Summoning every ounce of courage I had, I confronted Ty and delivered an ultimatum – he had to leave. Not just the house, but New Orleans altogether. It was a difficult decision, but one I knew was necessary to protect my children from further harm. Ty begrudgingly agreed to return to Miami, where he had come from.

However, there was a logistical hurdle to overcome – Ty didn't have the funds to purchase a bus ticket back to Miami. In a moment of desperation, I turned to my auntie Pam for help. With a heavy heart, I explained the situation to her, knowing that I couldn't bear to see my kids suffer any longer.

Thankfully, my auntie Pam was understanding and supportive. Without hesitation, she agreed to purchase a bus ticket for Ty, providing him with the means to return to Miami. It was a weight off my shoulders, knowing that I had made the right decision for my family's safety and well-being.

A few days later, Ty boarded the bus bound for Miami, leaving behind a trail of mixed emotions in his wake. While there was a sense of relief that the chaos and turmoil had come to an end, there was also a pang of sadness at the dissolution of our relationship. Despite everything, there had been moments of joy and happiness amidst the chaos, and it was hard to let go of those memories.

As Ty's bus pulled away, I couldn't help but feel a sense of trepidation about the road ahead. With Ty gone, the responsibility of raising our children fell squarely on my shoulders. It was a daunting prospect, but one I was determined to face head-on.

In the days that followed, my children struggled to come to terms with their father's absence. They cried and mourned the loss of his presence in their lives, and it broke my heart to see them in pain. But I did my best to comfort them, reassuring them that everything would be okay and that they were loved more than they could ever imagine.

As Ty left and the dust settled, I hoped that things would improve between my family and me. However, it seemed like the opposite happened. My auntie, who had once been a constant presence in our lives, began to distance herself from us. Instead of spending time with me and the kids, she would disappear early in the morning and not return until late at night. It was as if she was intentionally avoiding us, seeking refuge in the company of others.

My daughter, who was incredibly perceptive for her age, noticed the change in my auntie's behavior. She questioned why my auntie never visited us anymore, why she preferred to spend time at Auntie Ursula's house instead. It was a difficult conversation to have, as I struggled to find an explanation for my daughter's innocent inquiries.

Despite the hurt and disappointment I felt, I tried to shield my children from the harsh realities of our situation. I didn't want them to feel the pain of rejection or the sting of isolation. But deep down, I knew that they were feeling the effects of our strained relationships with our family members.

It was especially tough during special occasions like birthdays and family gatherings when we were left out of the celebrations. I had hoped that with Ty out of the picture, things would improve, but it felt like we were more alone than ever before.

Despite the challenges we faced, there was a glimmer of pride and joy in my heart when I learned that my daughter was gifted. Despite all the hardships we had endured, she had thrived and excelled beyond expectations. It was a testament to her resilience and strength, and it filled me with pride as a mother.

As my children grew older, they began to ask more questions about our family dynamics and why we were treated differently. It was a tough conversation to navigate, but I did my best to reassure them that they were loved and valued, regardless of the actions of others.

As time went by, Ty reached out, wanting to maintain a relationship with his children. He would call them regularly, and sometimes they even video chatted, which always brought joy to my children's faces. Hearing them excitedly exclaim, "Daddy's calling!" was heartwarming, and I was grateful that they could still connect with their father, even if it was only over the phone.

Despite Ty's absence, I promised him that once he got back on his feet in Miami, I would consider bringing the kids to visit him. It was important to me that they maintained a relationship with their father, despite the distance and challenges we faced.

Meanwhile, I found solace in spending time on the porch, chatting with a neighbor who knew my family well. Although he struggled with drug addiction, he always had kind words for me, praising me for being a good mother and keeping my kids well cared for. Our conversations provided a brief escape from the challenges of daily life, and I tried to offer him support and guidance whenever I could.

As time passed, I completed my hospitality course at the community college, and my graduation day arrived. My auntie, sister, uncle, and kids all attended the ceremony. However, the atmosphere was tense, and there was an uncomfortable silence between my sister and me throughout the car ride to the event.

Despite the lack of communication, I felt proud as I walked across the stage to receive my diploma. It was a significant achievement, and I was grateful to have my family there to witness it. However, once the ceremony was over, everyone went their separate ways, leaving me feeling lonely and saddened by the lack of connection between us.

After graduation, life continued with its ups and downs. I focused on being the best mother I could be for my children, despite the challenges we faced. Ty remained in Miami, struggling with homelessness, but he continued to stay in touch with the kids, providing them with some sense of stability amidst the uncertainty.

Meanwhile, my relationship with my auntie remained strained, as she continued to distance herself from me and the kids. It was disheartening to see our family ties unraveling, but I remained determined to provide a loving and supportive environment for my children, no matter what.

After my graduation, I felt a mix of emotions. While I was proud of my accomplishment, I couldn't help but feel a sense of disappointment that my family didn't celebrate the way other families did. Nevertheless, I focused on the positive and took my kids to the park to celebrate ourselves. I couldn't help but think of my mom and how proud she would have been of me for not only getting my GED but also graduating from college.

With my diploma in hand, I was determined to enter the workforce. I landed a job on a boat, working in hospitality as a line server. Eventually, I was promoted to manager, which was a great achievement for me. The job involved hosting two-hour cruises where people could sightsee and enjoy meals onboard. Sometimes, I had to work late, so I relied on my auntie and uncle to help with the kids, and they were always there for me.

My uncle became a father figure to my son, and they formed a close bond that warmed my heart. My uncle genuinely enjoyed spending time with the kids, and it brought me joy to see them together. However, tragedy struck when my uncle passed away. He had been feeling weak for some time, but his sudden death took us all by surprise.

The news hit us hard, especially my children, who had developed a close relationship with him. Unlike my mom and grandma, whom they barely remembered, they had fond memories of their uncle and felt his loss deeply. We gathered at his house, surrounding him with love in his final moments.

It was a difficult time for all of us, but we leaned on each other for support. After my uncle's passing, I felt a profound sense of loss. He had been my rock during the chaos with Ty, always supporting me without judgment. He was the only family member who stood by me through it all, never saying a bad word and always taking my side. I missed him dearly, especially his love for my kids and the time he spent with them, which no one else in the family seemed to do.

His death hit me hard, and I found myself turning to old habits to cope. My neighbor, Brian, whom I had grown close to, became a source of comfort for me. We would talk, and sometimes he would provide me with weed. Despite warnings from my auntie, who saw me talking to Brian on the porch, I trusted him. I knew he was going through his own struggles, just like me, and I valued his friendship.

Even though my auntie kept her distance because she didn't want me getting high, I continued to rely on Brian for support. I trusted him with tasks like picking up food for the kids, believing that he wouldn't take advantage of me, despite his drug use. I saw the good in him and valued our friendship.

As time passed, my dependence on Brian grew, and we spent more time together. He became a constant presence in my life, someone I could confide in and rely on. Despite the warnings from others, I knew that Brian was a good person, and I trusted him completely.

However, as my relationship with Brian deepened, I began to realize that my dependence on him was unhealthy. While he provided me with comfort and support, I knew that I needed to find healthier ways to cope with my struggles. I couldn't continue to rely on drugs or anyone else to numb my pain.

With this realization, I made the decision to distance myself from Brian and focus on finding healthier coping mechanisms. It wasn't easy, as he had become a significant part of my life, but I knew it was necessary for my well-being and the well-being of my children.

I sought support from other sources, reaching out to friends and family members who were willing to help me through this challenging time. I also started attending therapy sessions, where I could talk openly about my struggles and work towards healing.

Through therapy, I learned new coping strategies and ways to manage my emotions without turning to drugs. I also began to rebuild my relationship with my family, seeking their support and guidance as I navigated this difficult journey.

Brian went to get chicken for us, and he even returned my card afterward. He was always so kind. It was his birthday, and I remembered I had bought a chocolate cake while grocery shopping. I gave him a slice of cake, and he was so grateful. He hugged me and said thank you because nobody had ever given him anything for his birthday before. Everyone in the neighborhood treated him like he was nothing because of his situation. But I didn't judge him. I got to know him, and I understood why he was going through what he was going through.

A few days later, I was scrolling through Facebook, looking for Brian because I hadn't seen him in a while. I was worried about him. That's when I saw a post from his sister saying she would always miss him. I found out that Brian had overdosed and passed away. It hit me hard because he had been helping me through the loss of my uncle, who had also passed away recently. Brian knew my uncle, and we used to talk about what a good man he was.

When I found out about Brian's passing, it was really tough for me. He had been a source of comfort and support during a difficult time, and I missed him dearly. The next day, my auntie heard about Brian's death from a neighbor. It was a sad time for all of us. Brian may have had his struggles, but he was a good person who deserved better. His kindness and friendship meant a lot to me, and I would always remember him fondly.

Losing Brian made me realize how much I missed having someone to talk to, someone who understood what I was going through. It was hard to go back to feeling alone again, especially after having someone like Brian in my life. But I knew I had to keep moving forward for myself and my children. So, I leaned on my family for support and tried to focus on the good memories I had with Brian.

Despite the sadness of losing Brian, life went on. I continued working on myself, attending therapy sessions, and finding healthier ways to cope with my emotions. It wasn't easy, but I was determined to overcome my struggles and create a better life for me and my kids. With the love and support of my family, I knew I could get through anything that came my way.

After Brian passed away, it was tough for me. He had been a real support during the loss of my uncle. We used to talk about my uncle and how good of a person he was. Losing them both hit me hard. The next day, my auntie found out about Brian's passing from a neighbor. When she came to tell me, she said something negative about Brian, even though she didn't really know him. All she knew was that he had struggles with drugs. But Brian was more than that to me. He was a friend, the only friend I had at the time. Her negative comment upset me, and I asked her to give me back the spare key she had to my house. I didn't want her coming in whenever she felt like it anymore.

After that, my auntie kept her distance for a while, and it affected the kids too. But I was dealing with a lot at the time—grieving for both my uncle and my friend. When my uncle passed away, I had to slow down on my job, so I wasn't working at the time. I decided I wanted to do something different, so I enrolled in more classes. This time, I chose to study CNA, which is like working in a nursing home or being an in-home nurse. I've always wanted to help people, so this class felt like the right choice for me. It was only three weeks long, but it was intense.

During those three weeks, I learned a lot about caregiving and providing support to those in need. It felt fulfilling to be learning something new and meaningful. And even though it was challenging, it was worth it because I knew I was working toward a career where I could make a difference in people's lives. My kids were proud of me for taking on this new challenge, and it gave me the motivation to keep pushing forward, even when things got tough.

After completing the CNA course, there was a test to take, and once you passed, you got your certificate. So I went through that process, and I actually passed the test and received my certificate. There wasn't a big graduation ceremony or anything like that since it was just a three-week class. But having that certificate meant a lot to me. It was a validation of all the hard work I had put in.

With my new certifications in hospitality and CNA, I started looking for job opportunities in those fields. Eventually, I landed a job at a nursing home, which worked out well for me because the hours were flexible. I made sure to let them know that I had kids and needed to be home around the same time they got off the bus. It was a relief not to have to rely on my auntie for help with childcare anymore. Finally, things were starting to look up for me.

Then, out of the blue, Ty reached out to me. It had been almost a year since he had seen the kids, and he asked if they could come to Miami to visit him. Despite everything that had happened between us, I agreed. The kids missed their dad, and I thought it would be good for them to spend some time together. So we packed our bags and headed to Miami for a week.

When we got there, I was shocked to find out that Ty was homeless. He hadn't mentioned anything about it before we arrived. He did have a job washing cars, but he said he was sleeping at his job because he didn't have a place to stay. It was a tough situation, but I let him spend time with the kids at the hotel where we were staying. They were overjoyed to see their dad, and it warmed my heart to see them together.

During that week, there were no arguments or disagreements. Ty knew I would be heading back home soon, so he made the most of the time he had with the kids. They did activities together and just enjoyed being a family for a little while. But when the week was up, it was time for me and the kids to return to New Orleans.

After returning to New Orleans, I dove back into the workforce, balancing work and taking care of my kids. But deep down, I remembered the words of wisdom my grandma had shared with me about the importance of education. Despite the challenges I had faced and the struggles I had overcome, I realized that there were still opportunities for me to pursue my dreams. Inspired by my grandma's advice, I made the decision to further my education.

I enrolled in college once again, this time focusing on obtaining a Child Development Associate (CDA) credential. With a CDA, I could pursue a career working with children, either as a teacher or in early childhood education. The thought of working with kids filled me with excitement and anticipation. So I embarked on my journey to earn my CDA, quitting my job to focus on my studies while still receiving government benefits to support my family.

The road to earning my CDA was challenging. Classes were a mix of in-person sessions and online coursework, requiring me to juggle my studies with my responsibilities as a mother. But I remained dedicated and committed, determined to achieve my goal. After eight months of hard work and perseverance, I successfully earned my CDA.

Armed with my certificates, I began the search for employment in an in-home daycare setting. However, the job hunt proved to be more difficult than I had anticipated. Despite having the necessary qualifications, I faced challenges during interviews due to my speech impediment and lack of job experience. It was disheartening to feel judged based on factors beyond my control.

I want to express my gratitude to Miss Amy, who gave me my first job when no one else would hire me. Although it was an exciting opportunity, I knew I wanted to pursue a career working with children. Eventually, my perseverance paid off when Miss Lisa offered me a job at her in-home daycare. It was a moment of triumph, knowing that someone believed in me and my abilities.

Working in the in-home daycare was a wonderful experience for me. I enjoyed being around the kids and helping them learn and grow. But even though things were going well at work, I still struggled with my feelings of grief and sadness. It was a tough time for me, but I found comfort and strength in returning to my faith.I decided to start going back to church and introduce my kids to the teachings of Christianity. It was something I had grown up with, but had drifted away from in recent years. At first, I was angry with God for everything that had happened in my life, but I soon realized that everything happens for a reason. Returning to church helped me rediscover my sense of purpose and identity.

As I became more involved in church activities, I was asked to serve as an usher, just like my grandma had done when I was a child. It was a great honor for me to follow in her footsteps. Eventually, I even started preaching at the church. Despite my struggles with my speech impediment, the members of the congregation encouraged me to embrace my calling and share my message with others.

Going back to church and reconnecting with my faith helped me find peace and acceptance. I was grateful for every blessing in my life, especially considering the close calls I'd had in the past. I felt like I had finally found myself and learned to love and appreciate who I was.

As I continued to attend church with my kids and work at the daycare center, they were growing up fast. By the time I completed my CDA certification, they were around six or seven years old. They started asking more questions about life and the world around them, and I did my best to answer them honestly and thoughtfully.

After working at the daycare center for about six or seven months, I felt a longing to pursue another passion of mine: business. I wanted to start my own business someday, As I delved into my studies in business, I knew I would need some assistance with the kids, especially when it came to picking them up from school. Luckily, my auntie Pam stepped in to offer her support. Despite our past differences, she expressed her pride in me and acknowledged the effort I was putting into building a better future for my children.

With her help, I could focus on my college studies, knowing that my kids were in good hands.

With Auntie Pam watching over the kids, I was able to fully immerse myself in my pursuit of a business degree. It was a challenging journey, but I was determined to see it through. As I attended classes and completed assignments, I often thought about how far I had come and how much I had overcome. Each step forward was a testament to my resilience and determination to succeed.

Amidst my studies, my son Tyrone reached a significant milestone. He had been growing and maturing, and I could see him becoming more independent with each passing day. It was a proud moment for me as a mother to witness his growth and development. Tyrone's progress served as a reminder of the importance of perseverance and hard work, qualities that I hoped to instill in all my children.

As Tyrone continued to flourish, I found myself reflecting on the journey that had brought us to this point. It hadn't been easy, but it had been worth it. Despite the challenges and setbacks, I had never given up on my dreams or my children. And now, as I pursued my business degree, I knew that I was setting an example for them – showing them that with dedication and determination, anything is possible.

My days were busy, filled with classes, assignments, and caring for my children. But amidst the busyness, I always made time for family and faith. We continued to attend church regularly, finding solace and strength in our shared beliefs. The support of our church community bolstered us through the tough times and celebrated with us during the good times.

As the months passed, I drew closer to completing my business degree. However, unforeseen challenges arose, including the impact of COVID-19, which disrupted my studies. Despite my efforts, I was unable to finish the degree due to the pandemic and other life circumstances. Although disappointed, I remained resilient and focused on other areas of growth and development.

With the challenges posed by COVID-19, I faced uncertainty about the future and the path ahead. Yet, amidst the adversity, As I reflected on my journey, I realized that every obstacle had been a stepping stone, leading me closer to my dreams. And as I looked ahead to the future, I knew that no matter what challenges lay ahead, I would face them with the same determination and resilience that had brought me this far.

Chapter 13:
Navigating Through the Pandemic

When COVID-19 hit, it felt like the world came to a standstill. Everything shut down, and uncertainty hung heavy in the air. I remember those days vividly, when news of the pandemic spread like wildfire, and life as we knew it changed in an instant.

At that time, I was working on a boat, trying to make ends meet like always. But amidst the hustle and bustle of work, the news of the impending shutdown didn't register with me at first. I was so focused on my job that I didn't pay much attention to what was happening outside.

It wasn't until my last day on the boat that reality hit me. As I finished my shift and prepared to head home, my manager, Miss Amy, delivered the news that would alter our lives indefinitely. The boat was closing down, at least for the next two weeks, they said. Little did we know then, those two weeks would stretch into months of uncertainty.

That evening, as I left work and checked my messages, the full extent of the situation became clear. My kids' teachers were urging us to pick up their schoolwork immediately, warning that schools would be closed indefinitely. It was a scramble to gather their assignments and prepare for the unknown ahead.

In the midst of the chaos, there was a mix of emotions. Part of me welcomed the break from the relentless work schedule I had been maintaining. Working double shifts from morning till night had taken its toll, and I longed for a mental reprieve. But at the same time, I worried about how I would manage financially with everything shutting down.

The sudden change in routine was a welcome surprise for my kids, though. They were thrilled at the prospect of staying home from school and spending more time with me. And despite the uncertainty looming over us, those early days of lockdown were filled with precious moments of family time.

As the weeks turned into months, navigating through the pandemic brought its own set of challenges. Financial worries weighed heavily on my mind, as I grappled with how to keep up with bills and expenses without a steady income. But through it all, I remained grateful for the extra time I had with my children, cherishing the moments we shared together.

Despite the hardships, there were silver linings to be found amidst the chaos. The enforced slowdown allowed me to reconnect with my kids in ways I hadn't thought possible. We spent hours playing games, cooking together, and simply enjoying each other's company.

And amidst the uncertainty, there was a glimmer of hope as communities came together to support one another. Neighbors checked in on each other, offering help and kindness in times of need. It was a reminder that even in the darkest of times, there is strength in unity.

As the months stretched on, we adapted to the new normal as best as we could. Remote learning became our reality, with makeshift classrooms set up at home and Zoom calls replacing face-to-face interactions. It wasn't easy, but we persevered, finding ways to make the most of a challenging situation.

My kids struggled to stay focused during online classes, often getting distracted by the comforts of home. Without the structure of a traditional classroom setting, it was difficult for them to maintain their attention for extended periods.

I vividly remember the frustration of trying to keep them on track, only to find them dozing off or daydreaming during lessons. It was a constant battle to keep them engaged and motivated, especially my son, who was prone to getting sidetracked easily.

Despite my best efforts to provide a conducive learning environment at home, the distractions were endless. From the lure of toys to the allure of television, it seemed like there was always something vying for their attention. And as the weeks turned into months, the struggle to balance work, household chores, and homeschooling became increasingly overwhelming.

But amidst the chaos, there was a glimmer of hope in the form of financial assistance. When my coworkers reached out to inform me about the additional unemployment benefits available, it was like a weight lifted off my shoulders. The extra financial support provided some much-needed relief from the constant worry about bills and expenses.

The prospect of receiving additional funds through unemployment benefits brought a sense of stability and security during uncertain times. It was a lifeline for many of us who were struggling to make ends meet amidst the economic downturn caused by the pandemic. And while the situation was far from ideal, knowing that there was some financial support available provided a sense of reassurance.

As I navigated through the process of applying for unemployment benefits, I was met with both relief and frustration. Relief, because the extra funds would help alleviate some of the financial strain we were facing. But frustration, because the bureaucracy and red tape involved in accessing those benefits added an additional layer of stress to an already challenging situation.

But despite the hurdles, I persevered, determined to secure the financial assistance my family desperately needed. And when the first unemployment payment came through, it was a moment of immense relief and gratitude. The additional funds provided a much-needed buffer against the uncertainties of the pandemic, allowing us to breathe a little easier knowing that our basic needs would be met.

With the financial burden eased, I was able to focus more on supporting my kids through remote learning and navigating the challenges of daily life during lockdown. We established a routine that worked for us, carving out dedicated time for schoolwork, chores, and family activities.

And as we adjusted to the new normal, I found solace in the simple moments of togetherness that brought us closer as a family. From baking cookies together to backyard picnics, we made the most of our time at home, cherishing the silver linings amidst the uncertainty.

As the weather warmed and restrictions eased slightly, we ventured outside cautiously, grateful for the opportunity to stretch our legs and soak in some sunshine. But even these simple outings were tinged with anxiety, as the fear of contracting the virus loomed over us like a dark cloud.

I remember one incident vividly, when a trip to the grocery store turned into a confrontation with a fellow shopper. In the aisles crowded with anxious shoppers, tensions ran high as everyone tried to maintain the recommended six feet of distance. And when I inadvertently encroached on someone's personal space, I was met with hostility and aggression.

The encounter left me shaken and disheartened, highlighting the divisiveness and paranoia that had permeated society in the wake of the pandemic. It was a stark reminder of the fear and uncertainty that gripped us all during those tumultuous times.

But amidst the fear and uncertainty, there were moments of clarity and connection that buoyed our spirits. Despite our physical isolation, we found ways to stay connected with loved ones through phone calls, video chats, and socially distanced visits.

And while the threat of the virus loomed large, I held onto a steadfast belief in the power of faith and community to see us through. Despite the dire predictions and grim headlines, I refused to succumb to fear, choosing instead to trust in a higher power to guide us through the storm.

When my daughter Maya fell ill, I faced a moment of reckoning as a parent. The fear of taking her to the hospital amidst a raging pandemic was palpable, as stories of overwhelmed healthcare systems and misdiagnoses filled the airwaves.

But I relied on the wisdom and guidance of trusted friends and coworkers, who shared their own experiences and offered reassurance in the face of uncertainty. Together, we navigated the complexities of healthcare in the midst of a pandemic, relying on our instincts and intuition to guide us through.

And when Maya's illness turned out to be nothing more than a common cold, I breathed a sigh of relief, grateful for the power of community and connection to provide comfort and support during trying times. It was a reminder that even in the darkest of times, we are never truly alone.

As the pandemic dragged on, testing our resilience and resolve, I found solace in the simple moments of everyday life. From family dinners to movie nights at home, we cherished the moments of togetherness that brought us closer as a family.

And as we navigated the uncertainties of life in a pandemic, I held onto hope for a brighter future. A future where the world would emerge from the shadows of the pandemic stronger, more resilient, and more compassionate than ever before.

As the days passed, the rhythms of our lives shifted in unexpected ways. Each day brought new challenges and uncertainties, but also moments of resilience and strength.

When my daughter fell ill, I faced a moment of reckoning as a parent. The fear of taking her to the hospital amidst a raging pandemic was palpable, as stories of overwhelmed healthcare systems and misdiagnoses filled the airwaves. But I relied on the wisdom and guidance of trusted friends and coworkers, who shared their own experiences and offered reassurance in the face of uncertainty.

Together, we navigated the complexities of healthcare in the midst of a pandemic, relying on our instincts and intuition to guide us through. And when Maya's illness turned out to be nothing more than a common cold, I breathed a sigh of relief, grateful for the power of community and connection to provide comfort and support during trying times.

As the pandemic dragged on, testing our resilience and resolve, I found solace in the simple moments of everyday life. From family dinners to movie nights at home, we cherished the moments of togetherness that brought us closer as a family.

But even as we adapted to the new normal of life during a pandemic, uncertainty loomed on the horizon. When my manager, Miss Amy, reached out to me about returning to work on the boat, I faced a difficult decision. Despite the financial security offered by unemployment benefits, I grappled with the prospect of returning to work amidst ongoing concerns about the virus.

I chose to prioritize the safety and well-being of my family, opting to continue receiving unemployment benefits rather than returning to work on the boat. It was a decision fraught with uncertainty, but one that ultimately provided peace of mind in the midst of chaos.

And as the months wore on and the situation began to improve, albeit slowly, I faced another difficult decision as a parent. With the option to send my children back to school or continue with remote learning, I weighed the risks and benefits carefully, knowing that the choice would have far-reaching implications for their education and well-being.

I chose to keep my children at home for another two months, wary of the risks posed by returning to in-person learning amidst an ongoing pandemic. It was a decision made out of love and concern for their safety, but one that came with its own set of challenges and uncertainties.

As the pandemic gradually receded and life began to return to some semblance of normalcy, I found myself reflecting on the lessons learned during this tumultuous time. From the importance of community and connection to the resilience of the human spirit, the pandemic had taught me valuable lessons about what truly matters in life.

As the months passed and the seasons changed, life gradually began to regain a sense of normalcy. With each passing day, the world around us seemed to open up a little more, offering glimpses of hope and possibility in the midst of uncertainty.

For my children, returning to school marked a significant milestone in their journey through the pandemic. Despite the challenges of wearing masks and adhering to strict safety protocols, they embraced the opportunity to reconnect with their classmates and teachers, finding solace in the familiar rhythms of school life.

But for me, the prospect of returning to work on the boat remained a distant reality. Despite the gradual reopening of businesses and the easing of restrictions, I hesitated to reenter the workforce, wary of the risks posed by the ongoing pandemic.

For nearly a year, I had relied on unemployment benefits to provide for my family, grateful for the financial security it afforded us during uncertain times. But as the payments began to taper off and the pressure to return to work mounted, I found myself grappling with conflicting emotions and uncertainties.

On one hand, the thought of returning to work offered a sense of normalcy and routine in an otherwise chaotic world. But on the other hand, the fear of contracting the virus and putting my family at risk weighed heavily on my mind, leaving me torn between duty and self-preservation.

After much deliberation, I found myself at a crossroads, faced with the decision of whether to return to work or continue relying on unemployment benefits to sustain my family. As the payments began to dwindle, I knew that I couldn't put off the decision any longer.

Despite the financial strain, I hesitated to reenter the workforce, clinging to the newfound sense of freedom and flexibility that unemployment afforded me. For the first time in years, I had the opportunity to prioritize my well-being and spend quality time with my children, free from the constraints of a demanding job.

But as the weeks passed and the reality of our financial situation became increasingly apparent, I knew that I couldn't afford to remain idle forever. With bills piling up and expenses mounting, I knew that I had to make a choice, however difficult it may be.

In the end, it was a combination of financial necessity and a desire for stability that ultimately led me back to work. Despite my reservations, I knew that returning to the boat offered the best chance of providing for my family while minimizing the risks posed by the ongoing pandemic.

And so, after nearly a year of uncertainty and upheaval, I found myself once again navigating the familiar waters of the Mississippi, grateful for the opportunity to earn a steady income and support my loved ones in their time of need.

But the return to work was not without its challenges. With reduced hours and stringent safety protocols in place, life on the boat looked vastly different from the bustling, hectic days before the pandemic. Yet, despite the changes, I found solace in the routine and familiarity of my work, grateful for the sense of purpose it provided in an otherwise tumultuous time.

And as I settled back into the rhythms of life on the river, I found myself reflecting on the journey that had brought me to this point. From the uncertainty of those early days of the pandemic to the resilience and strength that carried me through, I knew that I had weathered the storm and emerged stronger on the other side.

For while the road ahead may still be uncertain, I know that I am not alone. With the support of my family, friends, and community, I am confident that we will overcome whatever challenges lie ahead, united in our determination to build a brighter, more hopeful future for ourselves and generations to come.

During the summer months, as the days grew longer and warmer, my focus shifted to ensuring that my children were staying on track academically despite the challenges posed by the pandemic. With their report cards in hand, I poured over the grades, mindful of any signs that they may have fallen behind during the tumultuous months of remote learning.

It was a relief to see that, despite the disruptions, they had managed to maintain their grades and keep up with their studies. Yet, lingering concerns remained about the impact of the pandemic on their education and their overall well-being.

But amidst the uncertainty, there were moments of joy and connection, particularly when it came to spending time with their father. Despite the physical distance between us, he made a concerted effort to stay involved in their lives, calling them regularly and making plans to visit whenever possible.

I remember one summer in particular when we embarked on a trip to Miami together, soaking up the sun and creating cherished memories that would last a lifetime. It was a much-needed break from the routine of daily life, a chance to relax and recharge amidst the backdrop of palm trees and ocean waves.

And as the years passed, we settled into a rhythm of co-parenting, navigating the challenges and joys of raising our children together, even as our lives took us in different directions. It was a testament to the enduring bond between us, a bond forged in love and commitment to our family.

But even as we embraced the joys of summer, the specter of COVID-19 loomed large, casting a shadow of uncertainty over our lives. With restrictions in place and social gatherings limited, we found ourselves adapting to a new normal, finding solace in the simple pleasures of life.

As the weeks into months, we found ourselves adjusting to the rhythms of life in the midst of a global pandemic. We took comfort in the small moments of connection, cherishing the time spent together as a family and finding strength in our shared resilience.

And as the world around us slowly began to reopen, we emerged from our isolation with a newfound sense of hope and gratitude. We embraced the opportunity to reconnect with loved ones, to rediscover the beauty of the world around us, and to forge ahead with renewed determination and purpose.

For while the road ahead may still be uncertain, we know that we are not alone. With each passing day, we are reminded of the power of resilience, the strength of community, and the enduring bonds of love that sustain us through even the darkest of times.

Chapter 14:
Building Friendships

As we strolled home from the park one day, I found myself reflecting on the connections I had made through social media. It was a source of positivity and encouragement, especially during the challenging times brought on by the pandemic. People from all over, including locals from New Orleans, would reach out with kind words and support, urging me to stay strong and keep my head held high.

During one encounter, a man approached me, calling out the nickname I used on social media. Initially taken aback, I soon realized he was addressing his son, whose name happened to be the same as my online alias. We struck up a conversation, exchanging phone numbers and introducing ourselves. His name was Matthew, and little did I know, this interaction would mark the beginning of a significant connection in my life.

At the time, I was focused on my journey of self-love and empowerment, hesitant to jump into a new relationship. Matthew, however, was persistent in his pursuit of friendship. Despite his eagerness, I made it clear that I needed time and space to heal from past experiences. To my relief, he respected my boundaries and embraced the opportunity to build a genuine connection based on mutual respect and understanding.

Matthew was a devoted father to his son, a quality that immediately caught my attention. We spent hours talking on the phone, sharing stories and getting to know each other on a deeper level. His sincerity and consistency were reassuring, providing me with a sense of stability during uncertain times.

As our friendship blossomed, Matthew invited me into his world, showing me glimpses of his life as a chef and a single parent. I admired his independence and work ethic, but I remained cautious, mindful of the importance of keeping our relationship grounded in friendship.

Despite the growing attraction between us, I was determined to prioritize my children and my own well-being. I had learned the hard way the consequences of rushing into relationships, and I was not willing to repeat past mistakes. My children looked up to me, and I knew they were watching my every move, learning from my example.

So, while Matthew's presence brought joy and companionship into my life, I made a conscious effort to maintain boundaries and proceed with caution. Our friendship served as a reminder of the importance of building meaningful connections based on trust, respect, and shared values.

Matthew's presence in my life brought a sense of stability and companionship during uncertain times. He was a man of integrity, dedicated to his work as a chef and his role as a father. Despite my initial reservations about getting involved in a new relationship, I found myself drawn to his genuine character and unwavering support.

As my friendship with Matthew deepened, I became more open to the idea of letting someone new into my life. However, I was determined to set a positive example for my children, especially my daughter. I wanted her to see the importance of independence and self-respect, showing her that she didn't need a man to define her worth.

My son, too, was watching closely, learning from my actions and the way I carried myself. I wanted him to understand the value of treating women with respect and equality, instilling in him the principles of kindness and empathy.

Matthew and I shared many meaningful conversations, both over the phone and in person. Despite our busy schedules, he made it a priority to check in on me regularly, offering words of encouragement and support. His commitment to our friendship was evident, and I appreciated his unwavering presence in my life.

As we spent more time together, I began to open up to Matthew about my past experiences and the challenges I had faced in previous relationships. He listened attentively, offering words of comfort and understanding. It was clear that he valued our connection and respected my boundaries.

One aspect of Matthew's life that stood out to me was his dedication to his work. He took pride in his role as a chef, pouring his heart and soul into every dish he created. His passion was infectious, and I admired his drive and determination to succeed.

Through social media, I shared snippets of our journey with my online community, affectionately referred to as my "Facebook family," "YouTube family," and "Instagram family." They offered words of encouragement and support, cheering us on as we navigated the ups and downs of life together.

Despite the challenges posed by the pandemic and the uncertainties that lay ahead, Matthew remained a constant source of strength and reassurance in my life. His friendship brought light into my world, reminding me of the power of connection and the importance of nurturing meaningful relationships.

My friendship with Matthew blossomed into something more meaningful over time. Despite my initial hesitations about getting involved in a new relationship, I found myself drawn to his genuine character and compassionate nature.

As we spent more time together, I couldn't help but admire Matthew's dedication to his role as a father. He was a loving and attentive dad to his son, despite the challenges they faced due to his son's health issues. Matthew's son suffered from seizures and required special care, but Matthew handled his responsibilities with grace and compassion.

One thing that stood out to me was the co-parenting dynamic between Matthew and his ex-partner. Unlike some situations I had encountered in the past, there was no drama or tension between them. They worked together seamlessly to ensure their son received the care and support he needed, setting a positive example for their child.

As our relationship progressed, Matthew's son became an integral part of our lives. I formed a bond with him, spending weekends together when Matthew had to work. Despite his health challenges, Matthew's son was a bright and spirited young boy, and I enjoyed watching him grow and thrive under his father's loving care.

Our blended family dynamic brought a sense of warmth and companionship into my life. My children got along well with Matthew's son, forming their own special bond. They played together, both indoors and outdoors, enjoying each other's company and creating lasting memories.

I appreciated Matthew's family-oriented nature, as he often included me in gatherings with his extended family. I had the opportunity to meet his cousins and other relatives, who welcomed me with open arms. It was heartwarming to see the love and support that surrounded Matthew and his son, and I felt grateful to be a part of their lives.

After about six months into our relationship, Matthew shared with me that he needed to find a new place to live. He explained that he wanted a bigger space for himself and his son, but he was hesitant to move because he valued our proximity to each other. Despite my initial reluctance to have another man move in with me, I suggested that he and his son move in with us.

This decision weighed heavily on me because I had made a promise to myself after my previous relationship that I wouldn't allow another man to live with me until we were married. However, I felt that

Matthew was a kind and responsible person, so I made an exception in his case.

When they moved in, I made sure to create a comfortable space for them in our home. His son visited every other weekend, so we set up a room for him with his own bed and belongings. I wanted him to feel welcome and at ease in his new surroundings.

In addition to adjusting to our new living arrangement, we also decided to invest in a car. While I didn't have a driver's license, Matthew did, but he had never been able to afford a car. Together, we pooled our resources, and I contributed most of the money towards purchasing a car. The car was registered in my name, but Matthew was added to the insurance policy, allowing him to use it for his daily commute to work.

Despite the challenges we faced, such as financial constraints and my lack of driving ability, we worked together to overcome obstacles as a team. Our relationship continued to strengthen as we navigated these challenges together, relying on each other for support and encouragement.

As Matthew settled into his role as a co-parent and partner, I was impressed by his dedication and commitment to our family. He took on additional responsibilities without hesitation, ensuring that both his son and I felt loved and cared for.

Our family outings with the car became a cherished routine. Matthew would drive us wherever we needed to go, whether it was to the nail salon for me or to run errands together. Despite the car needing some repairs, we were grateful for its reliability in getting us from one place to another.

My aunt, who lived next door, noticed our relationship and the addition of the car to our lives. She pointed out some of the car's flaws, like the worn-out seats and carpets, but we brushed off her concerns. We were more focused on the car's functionality rather than its appearance.

However, my aunt's energy towards our relationship didn't go unnoticed by Matthew. He questioned why she would make negative remarks, but I didn't delve into the details of my family history with him. I didn't want him to judge me or my aunt based on past experiences, especially since she lived nearby.

Despite any external challenges, our relationship continued to thrive. Matthew was dedicated to his work and committed to improving his financial management skills. He credited me with teaching him the importance of saving money, and he appreciated my independence and self-love journey.

In turn, I embraced his son as part of our family dynamic. I saw a reflection of myself in him and offered him guidance and support whenever he faced challenges. Whether it was dealing with bullies at school or building his self-confidence, I was there to lend a listening ear and words of encouragement.

As I spent more time with Matthew's son, I couldn't help but see myself in him—a younger version of myself navigating life's ups and downs. I felt a sense of responsibility towards him, wanting to instill in him the same values of resilience and self-assurance that I had learned over the years.

Our bond as a family grew stronger with each passing day. Things were going well with Matthew for the most part. We even discussed the topic of marriage, but I felt it was moving too fast for me. Marriage is a big step, especially when it comes to finances and sharing responsibilities. I wanted to make sure we were both ready for such a commitment.

Although I was open to the idea of marriage in the future, I made it clear to Matthew that I wasn't ready for it at the moment. He respected my decision and didn't bring it up again, which I appreciated. Despite this discussion, our relationship continued to flourish, and my kids grew fond of Matthew.

Matthew was wonderful with my children. He would play with them, chase them around the house, and even help out when I wasn't feeling well. There were times when I was sick, and Matthew would step in to pick the kids up from the bus stop for me. It meant a lot to me to have someone who was willing to step up and help out when needed.

He even took my son and his own son to the barbershop together, forming bonds and creating memories as a blended family. It felt like we were all one big happy family, and I couldn't have been happier with how things were going.

However, our relationship took a turn when I started going live on social media more frequently. Going live was something I enjoyed doing, as it allowed me to connect with people and share my thoughts and experiences. I viewed it as a way to build relationships and support each other through difficult times.

But Matthew began to feel jealous and insecure about my social media presence. He expressed concerns about my interactions with others online, especially since he had experienced jealousy in past relationships. I reassured him that my intentions were purely innocent and that going live was just a way for me to connect with my online community.

Despite my explanations, Matthew's jealousy persisted, causing tension in our relationship. He felt threatened by my interactions with others and worried that I might be forming emotional connections with people online. I tried to reassure him and alleviate his concerns, but it seemed like nothing I said could ease his jealousy.

As time went on, Matthew's jealousy became a source of conflict between us, and it began to take a toll on our relationship. I found myself having to choose between my passion for connecting with others online and maintaining harmony in my relationship with Matthew.

It was a difficult position to be in, torn between my desire to express myself freely and the need to address Matthew's insecurities. I realized that there were certain aspects that were causing me concern. One issue that arose was Matthew's reaction to my social media presence. While I enjoyed going live and connecting with my online community, Matthew began to express jealousy and discomfort with my interactions online. He felt threatened by the attention I received and worried that I might be forming emotional connections with others.

In an effort to appease him, I started going live less frequently, especially when he was around. However, I couldn't shake the feeling that I was compromising a part of myself for the sake of our relationship. It felt like I was sacrificing my authenticity to accommodate his insecurities.

source of tension in our relationship was Matthew's relationship with his ex-girlfriend and the mother of his child. While I understood that they needed to communicate for the sake of their son, I couldn't help but feel uneasy about their interactions. There were instances where Matthew seemed hesitant to introduce me to her, which left me feeling excluded and unimportant.

I confided in Matthew about my feelings, expressing my desire for more transparency and inclusion in his co-parenting arrangements. While he apologized and acknowledged his mistake, there were still moments where I felt like an outsider in his life.

One incident that particularly stood out to me was when Matthew hesitated to invite me to his son's surgery. He expressed concerns about how his ex-girlfriend would react to my presence, which left me feeling hurt and confused. It seemed odd to me that he would prioritize her feelings over mine, especially since she had moved on and remarried.

Despite my growing doubts and concerns, I tried to maintain faith in our relationship. Matthew was a good man who took care of our household and treated me and my children with kindness and respect. He contributed financially, cooked delicious meals, and was always there for us when we needed him.

However, as time passed, I couldn't shake the feeling that something wasn't right. I started to question Matthew's loyalty and commitment to our relationship, especially when I overheard him talking to his old friend about his past relationship with his ex-girlfriend. It made me wonder if he still harbored feelings for her or if there was more going on than he let on.

These doubts and uncertainties weighed heavily on my mind, causing me to reassess my feelings for Matthew. While I appreciated everything he had done for me and my children, I couldn't ignore the nagging feeling that our relationship was built on shaky ground.

As we stood in Walmart, arguing about his continued communication with his ex-girlfriend, I realized that I couldn't continue to overlook the red flags in our relationship. Despite my efforts to make things work, it was becoming increasingly clear that our relationship was no longer sustainable.

With a heavy heart, I knew that I needed to confront Matthew about my concerns and make some difficult decisions about the future of our relationship. It was a painful realization, but I knew that I needed to prioritize my own happiness and well-being, even if it meant walking away from someone I had once cared deeply about.

Chapter 15:
Facing Challenges

As I reflect on that tumultuous time in my life, I can't help but feel a mix of emotions—confusion, fear, and a sense of disbelief at what had transpired. It was a turning point in my relationship with Matthew, one that forced me to confront some harsh realities and make difficult decisions for myself and my children.

The incident at Walmart shook me to my core. It was the first time I had seen Matthew lose his temper in such a violent manner. His actions left me feeling scared and vulnerable, questioning whether I had made a mistake by allowing him into our lives. Despite his apologies and assurances that it would never happen again, I couldn't shake the feeling of unease that lingered in the air.

As Hurricane Ida approached, adding another layer of chaos to our already tumultuous situation, I found myself grappling with conflicting emotions. On one hand, I was terrified of the impending storm and the potential damage it could cause. On the other hand, I was faced with the harsh reality of my relationship with Matthew and the need to protect myself and my children from further harm.

In the midst of the chaos, Matthew suggested that we take a road trip to escape the storm and the stifling heat that accompanied the power outage. It was a spontaneous decision, but one that offered a temporary reprieve from the tension and uncertainty that had engulfed us.

As we packed our bags and piled into the car, I couldn't help but feel a glimmer of hope amidst the turmoil. Perhaps this road trip would offer us a chance to reconnect and rediscover the love and happiness that had once defined our relationship.

Driving down the open road, with the wind in our hair and the promise of adventure on the horizon, I felt a sense of freedom and liberation wash over me. For a moment, it was as if all our troubles had been left behind, replaced by the excitement of the unknown.

The kids were ecstatic, their laughter filling the car as we sang along to our favorite songs and played games to pass the time. It was a welcome distraction from the heaviness that had weighed us down in the days leading up to our impromptu escape.

As we journeyed further away from home, I couldn't help but marvel at the beauty of the world around us. The lush greenery, the rolling hills, and the endless expanse of sky seemed to stretch out before us, offering a sense of peace and tranquility amidst the chaos of our lives.

But even as we traveled farther from home, I couldn't shake the feeling of unease that gnawed at the edges of my mind. The events of the past few days had left me shaken and unsure of what the future held for me and my children.

As the miles passed by and the sun began to set on the horizon, I found myself lost in thought, grappling with the weight of the decisions that lay ahead. Would I have the strength to walk away from Matthew and start anew? Or would I continue to cling to the hope that things would somehow get better?

Deep down, I knew that I couldn't ignore the warning signs any longer. Despite his good qualities and the love he had shown me and my children, Matthew's actions had crossed a line that could not be undone. It was time for me to find the courage to stand up for myself and create a better future for me and my children, no matter how difficult it might be.

As we drove into the night, the road stretching out before us like a beacon of hope in the darkness, I made a silent vow to myself to never again allow anyone to treat me with anything less than the love and respect I deserved. It was a promise that I intended to keep, no matter what challenges lay ahead.

Returning home from our impromptu road trip to Arkansas, we were met with the harsh reality of life in the aftermath of Hurricane Ida. The power was still out, leaving us to swelter in the oppressive heat of the Louisiana summer. It was a stark contrast to the carefree days we had spent on the road, and the tension between Matthew and me hung heavy in the air.

Despite his attempts to make amends for his outburst at Walmart, I found myself growing increasingly wary of Matthew's behavior. His constant need to control my actions and dictate who I could talk to or what I could do only served to fuel my growing sense of unease.

As the days stretched on, with no end in sight to the power outage, Matthew returned to work, leaving me alone with my thoughts and fears. It was during these long, lonely days that I began to question the foundation of our relationship and whether it was built on a solid enough ground to withstand the challenges we faced.

With each passing day, the tension between us seemed to grow, fueled by his jealousy and my growing resentment towards his attempts to control me. I found myself withdrawing further and further into myself, seeking solace in the familiar routine of caring for my children and tending to the household chores.

But even as I tried to distract myself from the turmoil brewing beneath the surface, I couldn't shake the feeling that something was fundamentally wrong with our relationship. Despite his good qualities and the love he had shown me and my children, I couldn't ignore the warning signs any longer.

It was during one of our heated arguments that I finally found the courage to confront Matthew about his behavior. I told him in no uncertain terms that I refused to be controlled or dictated to by anyone, and that if he couldn't accept me for who I was, then perhaps it was time for us to go our separate ways.

His reaction was a mix of anger and frustration, but deep down, I knew that I had made the right decision for myself and my children. I couldn't continue to live in fear of his temper or his attempts to control me, no matter how much I cared for him or how much he had done for us in the past.

As the days turned into weeks, I began to make plans to leave Matthew and start anew. It wasn't an easy decision, but I knew that it was the only way for me to reclaim my sense of self and create a better future for myself and my children.

With the support of my friends and family, I began to take the necessary steps to extricate myself from the toxic relationship that had held me captive for far too long. It wasn't easy, and there were many obstacles along the way, but I refused to give up on myself or my children.

In the end, I found the strength to walk away from Matthew and the life we had built together. It wasn't easy, and there were many challenges along the way, but I knew that it was the right decision for me and my children.

As Christmas approached, the anticipation of meeting Matthew's parents filled me with both excitement and nerves. It would be the first time I had ever met a man's parents, and I wanted to make a good impression. Despite my nervousness, I was also eager to finally meet the people who had raised the man I loved.

Matthew's family was coming down from out of town to spend the holidays with us, and I found myself fretting over every detail, from what to wear to how to act. I wanted them to see me as the loving and caring partner that I strove to be for their son.

But there was another layer of complexity to the situation that added to my anxiety—Matthew's relationship with his ex, the mother of his son. They had known each other since they were teenagers, and their families were intertwined through years of friendship.

As Matthew's sister was best friends with his ex, it meant that their families had a close connection that extended beyond just co-parenting their son. This added an extra layer of pressure for me, as I worried about how his ex and her family would perceive me.

To make matters even more complicated, his ex was going through a divorce at the time, adding an extra layer of tension to the situation. I couldn't help but feel uneasy about the prospect of meeting her and navigating the delicate dynamics between her and Matthew's family.

Despite my apprehensions, I was determined to put my best foot forward and make the most of the situation. After all, this was an opportunity for me to show Matthew's family the love and respect that I had for their son, and I wasn't about to let my own insecurities stand in the way.

When the day finally arrived, I greeted Matthew's parents with a warm smile and open arms, doing my best to make them feel welcome in our home. It was a surreal experience, sitting down to dinner with them and exchanging stories and laughter as if we had known each other for years.

As the evening wore on, I found myself relaxing into the moment, enjoying the company of Matthew's family and feeling grateful for the opportunity to be a part of their lives. It was a stark reminder of the power of love and family to bridge the gaps between us and bring us closer together.

And while there were undoubtedly moments of tension and awkwardness, particularly when it came to navigating the dynamics between Matthew, his ex, and their families, I was determined not to let it overshadow the joy of the occasion.

Holidays passed without any major incidents, and I found myself feeling grateful for the chance to be surrounded by loved ones, both old and new. It was a time of reflection and growth, as I learned to navigate the complexities of family relationships and embrace the bonds that connected us all.

As we navigated through the intricacies of family dynamics, I found myself facing new challenges and emotions. Meeting Matthew's parents for the first time was an experience filled with both anticipation and uncertainty. Despite my nerves, I was determined to make a good impression and show them the love and respect that I had for their son.

However, things didn't quite go as smoothly as I had hoped. When Matthew's mom arrived in town, I was eager to meet her, but her initial reaction left me feeling hurt and misunderstood. She seemed dismissive and standoffish, brushing off my attempts to connect with her. It was a moment that shook my confidence and left me questioning my place in Matthew's life.

But I didn't let her reaction discourage me. Instead, I remained open-minded and willing to give our relationship a chance to grow. And as the days went by, I found myself forging a tentative bond with Matthew's family, one conversation and interaction at a time.

When the opportunity arose to meet Matthew's mom again, I seized it, determined to show her the kindness and warmth that I hoped would break through her initial reservations. And to my surprise, she responded positively, engaging in conversation and showing genuine interest in getting to know me and my children.

As we sat down to dinner together, I felt a sense of relief and gratitude wash over me. Despite the initial awkwardness, we had found common ground and were able to connect on a deeper level. It was a small victory, but it meant the world to me to know that I was accepted and welcomed into Matthew's family.

And as the holiday season approached, I found myself reflecting on the importance of family and the bonds that held us together. Despite our differences and past experiences, we were able to come together and celebrate the joy and love that filled our lives.

But amidst the festivities and celebrations, there were moments of doubt and insecurity that lingered in the back of my mind. As much as I wanted to believe in the strength of our relationship, there were still obstacles and challenges that we would need to overcome.

And so, as we embarked on this new chapter in our journey together, I couldn't help but wonder what the future held for us. Would we be able to overcome the challenges that lay ahead, or would our differences ultimately drive us apart?

Only time would tell, but one thing was certain—I was committed to facing whatever obstacles came our way, together. For better or for worse, we were in this together, navigating the complexities of love and family with open hearts and unwavering determination.

Chapter 16: Uncomfortable Revelations

The holiday season was in full swing, and one of Matthew's family members was hosting a Christmas party. It was also close to one of my parent's birthdays, adding to the festive atmosphere. Despite the excitement, my son had caught a cold and wasn't feeling well, so he stayed home with Auntie Pam while my daughter and I, along with Matthew and his son, attended the party.

As we arrived at the gathering, the warmth and cheer of the holiday spirit were evident. I knew a few of Matthew's family members, but not everyone. Despite this, they were welcoming and showed a lot of love to me and my daughter. However, the initial warmth soon gave way to a series of uncomfortable questions that caught me off guard.

Matthew's family members began asking about the father of my children. They were curious if my kids had the same father or different fathers. The repeated questions made me uneasy. I wasn't sure why they were so interested in my personal life, and it felt intrusive. Some of Matthew's cousins and even his mother asked me these questions. While they might have been trying to make conversation, their curiosity felt prying and judgmental.

In the midst of the party, I received a phone call from TY, who was asking about Tyrone and why he hadn't come to the party. The music was loud, so I stepped outside to take the call. During the conversation, I explained that Tyrone was sick and couldn't make it.

As I stood outside talking on the phone, I overheard a disturbing remark from one of Matthew's family members. They speculated that I was talking to another man, suggesting that I might be seeing someone else. This rumor quickly spread among the guests, and I could sense the discomfort it caused Matthew. He looked at me with suspicion, and I felt a growing tension between us.

The atmosphere became increasingly uncomfortable, and I began to feel out of place. The festive cheer was overshadowed by the judgmental glances and whispered rumors. I questioned why Matthew's family would make such assumptions and why they felt the need to interfere in our relationship.

As the evening wore on, my discomfort grew. I could see that Matthew was also affected by the rumors. His mood shifted, and he became distant. I was ready to go. Matthew's son wasn't very social. His disability made him uncomfortable around large crowds, much like me. I had never been comfortable in big groups either, and that became an issue in our relationship. Matthew was the opposite; he loved being around people, was the light of the party, and knew how to hold conversations effortlessly. I did not.

On the car ride home, the atmosphere was tense and awkward. Matthew's mom asked who I was talking to on the phone. I explained it was my child's father, not another man. After that, everyone in the car fell silent, making the ride home painfully awkward.

The next day, Matthew's parents went back out of town. Matthew drove them to the airport, and I noticed a change in him afterward. He became distant, and I could sense something was bothering him. I tried to get him to talk about it.

"Do you want to talk about anything that happened at the party?" I asked. "Something you didn't like?"

"No, I don't want to talk about anything. Everything is cool," he replied.

But things weren't cool. A few weeks later, when his parents called, he would go into the next room to talk to them. Before this incident, he always put us on the phone together, including the kids. It wasn't like that anymore. I got tired of the cold shoulder and confronted him.

He admitted he didn't like that I was on the phone with another man. He thought I was talking to someone from Facebook. I told him it was TY, but he didn't believe me.

"My whole family thinks I'm a fool for you," he said. "You went outside the whole time after that phone call. You didn't socialize with anyone, not even my mom."

I felt misunderstood and hurt. "I get so uncomfortable, Matthew, after what they said. It put a strain on our relationship."

Matthew's family members seemed to have formed negative opinions about me, and I could see it reflected in his actions. It made me feel alienated and judged. I wanted his family, especially his mom, to like me. I knew first impressions were everything, and I felt I had been unfairly judged for simply taking a phone call.

The situation affected our relationship deeply. Matthew's trust in me was shaken, and his family's opinions weighed heavily on him. He became more distant, and our interactions grew tense and strained. It felt like we were drifting apart, and I didn't know how to bridge the gap.

I tried to explain my feelings to Matthew, hoping to clear the air. "Matthew, I didn't mean to upset anyone. I just took a phone call. I was trying to be respectful by stepping outside. I didn't want to cause a scene."

But Matthew remained unconvinced. The damage was done, and his family's perception of me had tainted our relationship. I felt trapped in a cycle of mistrust and misunderstanding, unable to break free.

Days turned into weeks, and the tension persisted. I tried to focus on my children and keep things as normal as possible for them, but it was hard to ignore the growing rift between Matthew and me. I missed the closeness we once had, the easy conversations, and the laughter. Now, everything felt forced and distant.

Matthew's continued silence about the party incident only made things worse. He wouldn't talk about it, and his refusal to address the issue left me feeling helpless. I wanted to make things right, but I didn't know how.

I reached out to Auntie Pam for advice. She had always been a source of wisdom and support. When I told her about the party and the aftermath, she listened patiently.

"Sweetie, sometimes people make quick judgments without understanding the full picture," she said. "You need to keep communicating with Matthew, even if it's hard. Don't let this misunderstanding fester."

Encouraged by her words, I tried to talk to Matthew again. "Matthew, we need to talk about this. I don't want this misunderstanding to ruin what we have."

He sighed, looking weary. "I know, but it's not just about us. It's my family too. They think I'm blind to what's going on."

"But nothing is going on, Matthew. I love you and only you. Why can't they see that?"

He didn't have an answer, and the conversation ended in the same unresolved tension. I felt like we were stuck in a loop, unable to move forward.

As the weeks passed, I focused on rebuilding our trust. I made an effort to be more open and communicative, hoping that my actions would speak louder than words. I wanted to prove to Matthew that there was nothing to worry about, that our relationship was solid and worth fighting for.

Matthew slowly began to respond, but the process was slow and fraught with setbacks. His family's opinions still loomed over us, a constant reminder of the party and the misunderstandings that followed. It was hard to shake the feeling that we were being judged, that our relationship was under scrutiny.

But after that, he started to not invite us to stuff. They had a New Year's party, and one of his cousins was going to propose to his girlfriend. Matthew didn't ask if I wanted to go. He just said, "Oh, I know you probably don't want to go anyway. You know, you're not really going to be talking."

That really hurt. He thought I preferred talking on Facebook more than to people in real life. He felt it was easier for me to talk on social media because I didn't have to face anyone. He didn't understand that my struggle with talking to people was tied to my speech problems and what I went through growing up. I was very quiet as a child, and that carried into adulthood.

I tried to explain to him that it wasn't that I didn't like his family or didn't want to talk to them. It's just that I am a quiet person. I find it hard to hold conversations with people. When I do talk, I feel like I don't speak well, and people often give me looks. Even as an adult, people have made fun of the way I talk. It's something I've always struggled with.

This became a bigger issue between us. Matthew started sleeping on the couch. At first, I didn't think much of it. I thought he just fell asleep watching TV. But then I noticed a change in his routine. He would come home, not interact with the kids like he used to. He would ask me how my day was in a very routine way, not really listening to my response.

He would eat dinner and then go straight to the couch. I would invite him to watch TV with me in bed like we used to, but he would say, "No, I'm good on the couch." This hurt because we used to watch TV together and fall asleep next to each other.

I felt him slipping away. The warmth and connection we used to have were fading. Our conversations became short and formal, lacking the intimacy we once shared. I missed his laughter, his interest in my day, and his playful interactions with the kids.

One evening, I decided to confront him about it. "Matthew, why are you sleeping on the couch every night? We used to watch TV together. What happened?"

He sighed and avoided eye contact. "I just need some space," he said.

"Space? From what? From me?" I asked, feeling a lump in my throat.

"From everything," he replied. "I just need time to think."

His response was vague and didn't provide the clarity I was seeking. I felt a mixture of frustration and sadness. I didn't know how to fix what was broken because I didn't fully understand what was wrong. The distance between us grew, and I felt helpless.

Days turned into weeks, and the situation didn't improve. Matthew continued his routine of coming home, barely interacting with us, eating dinner, and retreating to the couch. The kids noticed the change too. They asked why Daddy didn't play with them as much anymore, and I didn't have a good answer for them.

I tried to keep things normal for the kids, but it was hard. I missed the man who used to light up the room with his presence, who made us laugh and feel loved. Now, it felt like he was just a shadow of himself, distant and unreachable.

I sought advice from Auntie Pam again. "I don't know what to do, Auntie. Matthew is so distant. He barely talks to me or the kids anymore."

But Pam wasn't much help. She was always busy with her own life, and our conversations lacked depth. So, I turned to Facebook instead. It became my sanctuary, a place where I could connect with others who understood what I was going through. One person, in particular, had a relationship I admired, and I found solace in talking to them.

However, even when Aunt Pam watched the kids for me, she didn't engage beyond the surface. She'd leave as soon as I returned, without asking about my day or showing any interest in how I was doing. It was disappointing and left me feeling even more isolated.

One night, after the kids were asleep, I sat beside him on the couch. "Matthew, we need to talk. I can't keep pretending everything is okay when it's not."

He looked tired and weary. "What do you want to talk about?"

"Us. Our relationship. I feel like we're drifting apart. You're not the same. I'm not the same. I miss us."

He sighed deeply. "I don't know what to say. Things have been hard."

"I know. But we need to work through it together. Please, let's try."

He nodded slowly. "I'll try."

It was a small step, but it gave me a glimmer of hope. We began to have more conversations, though they were still strained and uncomfortable at times. I tried to be more understanding and patient, hoping to rebuild the trust and connection we once had.

The journey was long and challenging. We had good days and bad days, moments of closeness and moments of frustration. But I held onto the hope that we could find our way back to each other. I believed in the love we shared and was determined to fight for it.

Slowly, things began to improve. Matthew started spending more time with the kids, playing and laughing with them like he used to. He began to open up to me more, sharing his thoughts and feelings. We started watching TV together again, finding comfort in each other's presence.

It wasn't easy, and it wasn't perfect. But we were trying. We were working through the misunderstandings and the hurt, rebuilding our relationship step by step. Then, when I started seeing him sleeping on the couch more often, maybe a week had passed, I confronted him again. I asked, "Why are you always sleeping on the couch? Don't you want to sleep in the bed with me anymore?" He replied, "No, I just want to sleep on the couch." I said, "Okay," and let it go.

But he kept doing it. Sometimes, he'd come to bed around one or two in the morning, trying to sneak in when he thought I was asleep. I noticed he was hiding his phone from me more often, which was unusual. One day, I walked up to him, and he quickly put his phone away. I didn't say anything at the time, but I thought it was strange. Matthew had never done that before. He was always open with his phone and said he had nothing to hide.

One night, when he was asleep, I decided to go through his phone to figure out what was going on. His behavior had been so different. When I looked, I found that he had downloaded a dating app and was messaging other women. He hadn't met up with anyone as far as I could see, but he was sending messages like, "Hey, how are you?" and "You look beautiful."

It was very hurtful to see that, especially since he hadn't been giving me any compliments. I confronted him about it, and of course, he got mad. He asked, "Why did you go through my phone?" I told him, "I went through your phone because you weren't telling me what was going on. I had to find out why your behavior changed."

He tried to justify his actions by saying, "Well, you're on Facebook messaging other men. It's the same thing I'm doing." I told him that Facebook isn't a dating website, and that's not what I use it for. We argued about it, and in my frustration, I kicked him out of the house. It was the weekend his son was supposed to come over, so he begged to come back, saying, "You can't do this to my son."

I let him come back for his son's sake, but he didn't really apologize. He just tried to sweep everything under the rug. I was left feeling betrayed and hurt. Our relationship was hanging by a thread, and I didn't know how to mend it.

After that, things were tense. We barely spoke, and when we did, it was mostly about practical matters concerning the kids or the house. The warmth and connection we once had felt like a distant memory. I missed the days when we laughed together and shared everything.

One evening, I tried to talk to him again. "Matthew, we need to talk about what happened. We can't just ignore it."

He sighed, looking weary. "What do you want to talk about? I already told you, there's nothing going on."

"There's clearly something going on," I insisted. "You were on a dating site, talking to other women. That's not nothing."

He shook his head. "I was just bored. It didn't mean anything."

"Bored?" I repeated, feeling a mix of anger and sadness. "Do you know how hurtful that is to hear? You weren't bored with me, you were just bored."

He didn't have an answer. He just looked away, avoiding my eyes. It was clear that he didn't want to have this conversation, but I couldn't let it go.

"We need to figure this out," I said, my voice softer now. "For the kids, for us. I can't keep living like this, Matthew."

He finally looked at me. "I don't know what you want me to say. I'm sorry, okay? I messed up."

His apology felt half-hearted, but it was a start. I decided to take it and try to move forward. Matthew acted like being on a dating website didn't bother him at all, and I saw this. I told him it was hurtful and made me feel like he didn't want me anymore. This became a major issue in our relationship. Even though I let him back in the house because his son was coming over, things remained awkward. He suggested we try not to argue, especially in front of his son, and I agreed.

However, I noticed a pattern. While he didn't want to argue in front of his son, he often picked fights with me when it was just me and my kids around. Small things would set him off, like dishes left in the sink. He would complain, "Why can't you wash the dishes?" I'd respond, "Matthew, it's two plates. If you want them washed, you wash them." This led to petty arguments that we never had before.

cope, I threw myself back into work. I felt our relationship was falling apart, and I didn't know what to do. Although he deleted the dating app, I couldn't let go of the fact that he went on it in the first place. I kept bringing it up because it felt like there was a deeper issue he wasn't addressing.

During the summer, his son started staying with us for longer periods, not just every other weekend. This created a problem for Auntie Pam, who watched my kids while I was at work. She was overwhelmed and would call me at work, complaining about the extra burden. Matthew also started bringing his cousin's son over to play with his own son, which added to Auntie Pam's stress.

I talked to Matthew about it, saying, "My auntie is having trouble watching your cousin. Can you handle it?" He felt like he wasn't part of the family because Auntie Pam always had something to say about his son and cousin. We didn't argue much about it; I just told him to discuss it with Auntie Pam directly.

Matthew often felt like he wasn't fully accepted in the family, which was a point of tension. Despite our issues, he was still very romantic, always buying me gifts for my birthday, Valentine's Day, and Christmas. Auntie Pam noticed this and once said, "I want a man who buys me gifts." For Valentine's Day, he gave me a beautiful rose, and she expressed envy over it.

Despite these romantic gestures, our relationship's cracks were widening. One evening, I decided to address our problems head-on. I said, "Matthew, we need to talk about us. We can't keep ignoring what's happening."

He looked tired but agreed. "What do you want to talk about?"

"Our relationship," I replied. "We're not connecting like we used to. You're distant, and I feel like you don't want to be with me anymore."

He sighed deeply. "I know. I've been feeling that way too. I don't know what to do."

"Can we at least try to fix this?" I asked. "For the kids, if not for us?"

He nodded. "Yeah, let's try."

We decided to see a counselor, hoping it would help us understand each other better. The sessions were tough, forcing us to confront painful truths. Matthew admitted he felt neglected and turned to the dating app for attention. I shared how his actions made me feel insecure and unwanted. We both had to take responsibility for our mistakes and work on rebuilding trust.

It was a slow process. We started communicating more openly and tried to reconnect as a couple. We went on dates, even simple ones at home after the kids were asleep. These small efforts helped us remember why we fell in love in the first place.

There were setbacks, of course. Old habits die hard, and sometimes we reverted to our previous behaviors. But we kept trying, knowing that our relationship was worth fighting for.

Despite the outward appearances of our relationship—gifts, dinners, and gestures of affection—the cracks were deepening. It was clear that things weren't as they seemed. People may see one thing, but the reality can be very different.

Matthew was struggling. He felt like he didn't fit into my life anymore, and I didn't know how to help him. Then, another incident added to the strain. His son's grandma, his mother's mother, passed away.

He didn't communicate with me about wanting to attend the funeral. Instead, he mentioned going to the repast, assuming I'd understand. It felt like he had a whole other life I wasn't a part of. He didn't even ask if I wanted to go, even though I had met the lady a few times and would have supported him and his son.

Just two days before the funeral, he mentioned needing an outfit. He'd lost all his money due to gambling, and he wanted me to buy him something to wear. I was upset that he hadn't told me sooner, but I helped him anyway.

When he returned from the funeral, he was distant, as if I were the problem. He didn't want to talk, so I gave him space. He was mourning, but his behavior towards me was hurtful.

He reminded me that his son had lost his grandma, as if my losses didn't matter. I reminded him that my children had lost their grandma too, and they didn't even have memories of her. It hurt that he seemed to dismiss my pain.

After that, our relationship spiraled further. We were both busy with work, and when we came home, the atmosphere was tense. Communication dwindled, and awkward silences filled the air. Matthew tried to discipline my son more than my daughter, which added to the tension.

It felt like we were living separate lives under the same roof. Despite our efforts to reconnect, our relationship continued to deteriorate. We were drifting further apart, and I didn't know how to bridge the gap.

Matthew's grief seemed to consume him, leaving little room for anything else. He was distant and withdrawn, and I felt helpless. I wanted to support him, but it felt like he didn't want my help.

I wondered if our relationship could survive this latest challenge. We had overcome so much already, but this felt different. The distance between us seemed insurmountable, and I didn't know if we could find our way back to each other.

As the days passed, the tension between us only grew. We tiptoed around each other, careful not to say the wrong thing. It was exhausting, and I longed for the closeness we once shared.

But no matter how hard I tried, I couldn't seem to reach him. He was lost in his grief, and I didn't know how to bring him back. Our relationship was a tangled mess of miscommunications and unresolved issues. Despite our efforts to reconnect, it seemed like we were drifting further apart with each passing day. Matthew's behavior towards my son became a point of contention. While I had agreed to discipline each other's children,

I never expected him to resort to physical punishment. It was a clear violation of our agreement and only added to the strain between us.

His demeanor had shifted dramatically from the loving, playful man I once knew. He withdrew into himself, leaving me feeling isolated and alone. I turned to social media for advice, desperate for a solution to our crumbling relationship. The responses were mixed, but many suggested that it might be time to let go.

Despite the doubts swirling in my mind, I was determined to give our relationship one last chance. We had a heart-to-heart, and Matthew promised to change his ways. For a brief period, things seemed to improve. He cooked, he talked, and he tried to reignite the spark between us. But it wasn't long before old habits resurfaced.

His increased communication with his ex only added to my unease. I couldn't shake the feeling that there was something more between them, despite his assurances to the contrary. Our arguments became more frequent, and tensions reached a breaking point one fateful day.

We were driving, arguing as usual, when suddenly Matthew began driving recklessly. His words cut through me like a knife as he threatened to end both our lives. It was a terrifying ordeal that left me shaken to the core.

When he dropped me home, I knew that there was no going back. The man I thought I knew was gone, replaced by someone I didn't recognize. It was a painful realization, but I knew that I couldn't stay with someone who had put my life in danger.

As Mardi Gras approached, tensions between us continued to simmer. His desire for more children only added fuel to the fire, sparking yet another argument. He accused me of lying about being on birth control, but I knew that bringing a child into our already fractured relationship would only make things worse.

Our relationship had become a rollercoaster of highs and lows, with no end in sight. Some days were filled with love and intimacy, while others were marred by bitter arguments. It was a cycle that seemed impossible to break, and I didn't know how much longer I could hold on.

As I prepared for work one day, the tension between us reached a boiling point. Matthew's jealousy over my auntie's relationship spilled over, leaving me feeling suffocated by his insecurities. It was a stark reminder of how far we had drifted apart.

At that moment, I knew that something had to change. I couldn't continue living in fear, tiptoeing around his moods and insecurities. It was time to take a stand and reclaim control of my life, even if it meant walking away from the man I once loved.

Chapter 17: Breaking Point

The tension between Matthew and me had reached a boiling point, and I knew that something had to give. As I prepared for work one day, Matthew's jealousy over my auntie's relationship spilled over, leaving me feeling suffocated by his insecurities. It was a stark reminder of how far we had drifted apart.

"I got to go to work," I announced, hoping to diffuse the situation.

But instead of understanding, Matthew erupted in anger. He insisted that it wasn't a good idea for the kids to be at my auntie's house while her partner was around. His irrational jealousy was becoming unbearable, and I had finally reached my breaking point.

"I'm tired of this relationship," I declared, my voice trembling with frustration. "I'm tired of you complaining about every little thing. We just need to break up."

Matthew's response was chilling. He didn't say a word, just stormed out of the house without a backward glance. I felt a pang of sadness, but I knew that ending things was the right decision.

As he left, I demanded my car keys, reminding him that I had paid for most of the car. His refusal only fueled my anger, and I made a snap decision to involve the police. It was a move born out of desperation, but I couldn't let him take away something that was rightfully mine.

When the police found him, they asked if I wanted to press charges, but I declined. All I wanted was my car keys back. Matthew's attempts to justify his actions fell on deaf ears. We were done, and I had no intention of getting involved in his problems any longer.

I knew that some people might see my actions as petty, but I couldn't let him walk all over me. It was a matter of principle, and I refused to back down. As I watched him drive away, a wave of relief washed over me. It was finally over.

But even as I reclaimed control of my life, doubts lingered in the back of my mind. Had I made the right decision? Was there more I could have done to salvage our relationship? It was a question that would haunt me for weeks to come.

In the days that followed, I found myself replaying our relationship over and over in my mind, searching for answers that never came. I couldn't shake the feeling that I had let both myself and Matthew down.

The aftermath of our breakup left me reeling with a mix of emotions. Selling the car that had been a symbol of my independence felt like a necessary step, but it was a painful reminder of everything that had gone wrong between Matthew and me.

I vividly remember the day I had to break the news to my children that Matthew wouldn't be around anymore. Their tears were like daggers to my heart, and I vowed then and there to shield them from any more pain.

It wasn't just me who was struggling in the wake of our breakup. Matthew had lost his job, and while part of me suspected that our relationship troubles had played a role, I couldn't help but feel a pang of sympathy for him. Despite everything, he was still a part of my past, and I couldn't shake the feeling that we had both lost something precious.

But as the days turned into weeks, I began to see a glimmer of hope on the horizon. The burden of our toxic relationship had been lifted, and I felt lighter, freer than I had in a long time. I knew that it was time to focus on myself and my children, to build a future that was rooted in love and stability.

Cutting ties with social media was a small sacrifice to make for my peace of mind. Matthew's insecurities had cast a shadow over our relationship, and I was determined not to let them hold me back any longer. It was a liberating feeling, reclaiming control over my own life.

As I settled into the rhythm of single parenthood, I rediscovered the joys of independence. I no longer had to walk on eggshells around Matthew, or tiptoe around his moods. I was free to be myself, unapologetically.

Of course, there were moments of loneliness and doubt. The memories of our time together lingered like ghosts, haunting me when I least expected it. But with each passing day, their hold on me grew weaker, until one day, they were little more than echoes of the past.

And as I watched my children grow and thrive in the absence of Matthew's toxic influence, I knew that I had made the right decision. My breakup with Matthew brought to light some uncomfortable truths about my family dynamics. While Matthew had been a supportive and caring partner, it seemed that not everyone in my family was happy to see us together.

My auntie Pam, in particular, had always been a source of tension in our relationship. Despite her outward displays of kindness, I couldn't shake the feeling that there was something insincere about her gestures.

It was only after Matthew came into my life that I began to notice a shift in her behavior. Suddenly, she was showering me with gifts and attention, as if trying to prove something to herself and to others.

But beneath the surface, I sensed a hint of jealousy lurking. Auntie Pam had never been one to share the spotlight, and it seemed that my newfound happiness with Matthew was threatening to overshadow her own.

And it wasn't just Auntie Pam who seemed to resent our relationship. Even my sister, who should have been celebrating my happiness, appeared distant and aloof.

I'll never forget the year when Matthew bought me a birthday cake and took me out to dinner. It was a small gesture, but it meant the world to me. Yet, when my own family couldn't be bothered to come inside and wish me a happy birthday, I couldn't help but feel a pang of sadness.

I found myself grappling with a new set of challenges, this time within my own family. The rift between me and my auntie Pam seemed to widen with each passing day, revealing a troubling dynamic that had been lurking beneath the surface all along.

It was strange how quickly things had changed once Matthew was out of the picture. Suddenly, my auntie's true colors began to show, and I realized that her kindness had always been conditional, contingent upon her own desires and insecurities.

The incident with my son, Tyrone, was a stark reminder of just how fragile our relationship had become. When I confronted her about neglecting to feed him, she brushed off my concerns with excuses and deflections, refusing to take responsibility for her actions.

But I wasn't about to let her off the hook that easily. I went live on social media to vent my frustrations, airing out the details of our family drama for all to see.

I was angry, hurt, and fed up with the way she had treated me and my children.

In the aftermath of our confrontation, I turned to Ty for support. Despite living out of town, he offered to check in on the kids while I was at work, providing a much-needed lifeline during a tumultuous time.

But even with Ty's help, I couldn't shake the feeling of unease that lingered in the air. My auntie's behavior had left a bitter taste in my mouth, and I couldn't help but question whether I could ever truly rely on her again.

As I continued to monitor the situation from afar, I grew increasingly wary of leaving my children in her care. The history of tension and resentment between us cast a long shadow over our relationship, and I couldn't help but wonder if her motives were driven more by a desire for control than genuine concern for our well-being.

And then there was Tori, my cousin's child, who seemed to have become a pawn in my auntie's game of manipulation. By taking him under her wing, she had effectively sidelined my own children, leaving them feeling neglected and abandoned.

The incident with Tori had been the last straw for me. It was clear that my auntie's favoritism towards him, coupled with her neglect of my own children, was a clear sign that things had gone too far.

I confronted her about it, demanding answers and asserting my right to set boundaries within my own home. But instead of acknowledging my concerns, she brushed them off, insisting that everything was fine and refusing to take responsibility for her actions.

It was a bitter pill to swallow, realizing that the person I had once trusted to have my back was now working against me. But I knew that I couldn't let her behavior go unchecked any longer.

So I made the difficult decision to quit my job and focus on taking care of my kids full-time. It wasn't an easy choice, but I knew it was the right one for me and my family.

But even with my newfound freedom, the tension between me and my auntie continued to simmer beneath the surface. Her refusal to respect my boundaries only served to exacerbate the situation, leaving me feeling even more isolated and alone.

I knew I had to take action. So I confronted her once again, demanding that she return the key to my house and respect my space and privacy.

It was a difficult conversation, filled with tension and frustration. But in the end, I stood my ground, refusing to back down until my demands were met.

And to my surprise, she relented, begrudgingly handing over the key and begrudgingly agreeing to respect my boundaries in the future.

It was a small victory, but it was a step in the right direction. For the first time in a long time, I felt like I had taken control of my life and my destiny, and I was determined to do whatever it took to protect myself and my children from any further harm.

As I settled into my new role as a full-time caregiver, I found solace in the simple moments of everyday life. Whether it was cooking dinner with my kids or snuggling up together on the couch, I cherished every moment we spent together, knowing that we were stronger together than we could ever be apart.

And as the days turned into weeks and the weeks turned into months, I began to see a glimmer of hope on the horizon. The wounds of the past were slowly healing, and I knew that with time and patience, we would emerge from this ordeal stronger and more resilient than ever before.

But until then, I would continue to stand firm in my resolve, knowing that no matter what challenges lay ahead, I would face them head-on with courage and determination. For me and my children, the future was bright, and nothing could stand in our way.

Chapter 18: Moving On

Leaving my auntie's house was a monumental step towards reclaiming my independence and creating a sense of privacy and security for myself and my children. It wasn't easy, but it was necessary for our well-being and peace of mind.

Securing Section 8 housing provided us with a stable foundation to build our new life upon. It was a relief to know that we had a place to call our own, free from the prying eyes and judgment of others.

Moving out of the familiar neighborhood where I had grown up was both liberating and bittersweet. While I cherished the memories we had made there, I knew that it was time to move on and start fresh somewhere new.

With the decision made to sell the family house, a chapter of my life came to a close. It was a bittersweet moment, saying goodbye to the place that held so many memories, both happy and challenging. But it was also a necessary step towards embracing a new beginning, one that was filled with promise and possibility.

Navigating the process of selling the house was not without its complications, given the shared ownership between my auntie and myself. However, with careful negotiation and legal arrangements, we were able to reach an agreement and move forward with the sale.

For my auntie, the sale of the house meant a significant change in her living situation. Without the security of the family home, she was forced to explore other options for housing, including seeking assistance from her sister, Ursula. It was a reminder of the fragility of our circumstances and the importance of having a stable and supportive environment to call home.

As for myself, the sale of the house marked the beginning of a newfound sense of independence. No longer tied to the expectations and dynamics of family life, I was free to chart my own course and create a home environment that reflected my values and aspirations.

The transition was not without its challenges, of course. Adjusting to life on my own, without the familiar presence of my auntie nearby, required a period of adaptation and self-discovery. But with each passing day, I grew more confident in my ability to navigate the ups and downs of single parenthood and independent living.

And while there were moments of loneliness and uncertainty along the way, there was also a profound sense of liberation and empowerment that came from taking control of my own destiny. I no longer relied on others to define my worth or dictate my path in life—I was the master of my own fate, and that was a truly empowering realization.

As I settled into my new life away from the chaos and drama of my family, I found a sense of peace and contentment that had long eluded me. With each passing day, I embraced the freedom and independence that came with being on my own, relishing in the opportunity to focus on myself and my children without the distractions of family drama and dysfunction.

Returning to work was a significant step forward for me, not just financially, but also emotionally and mentally. It gave me a sense of purpose and stability, allowing me to provide for my children and create a better life for us all. And while I initially hoped that my auntie would be able to help with childcare, I understood her limitations and adapted accordingly, finding a job that fit around my responsibilities as a single mother.

Being a single mom was no easy feat, but it was a role I embraced wholeheartedly. With each challenge that came my way, I faced it head-on with determination and resilience, knowing that I was doing everything in my power to give my children the best possible life.

Despite my efforts to maintain a relationship with my family, particularly my sister, I soon realized that our connections had become strained and one-sided. I found myself constantly reaching out, only to be met with silence or indifference on the other end. Eventually, I grew tired of the one-sided effort and decided to focus my energy on the relationships that truly mattered—those with my children.

And so, I forged ahead, finding strength and solace in the love and companionship of my children. Watching them grow and thrive brought me immeasurable joy and fulfillment, reminding me of the blessings that surrounded me each and every day.

Though there were moments of loneliness and longing for a supportive community to lean on, I refused to let those feelings consume me. Instead, I leaned into my independence and self-reliance, knowing that I was capable of overcoming any obstacle that came my way.

As time passed, I learned valuable lessons about resilience, perseverance, and the true meaning of family. I discovered that family isn't always blood, but rather those who stand by you through thick and thin, offering support and encouragement when you need it most.

As I reflect on my journey of single motherhood and independence, I've come to appreciate the freedom and self-discovery that comes with being unattached. Though there are moments of loneliness and longing for companionship, I find solace in the love and bond I share with my children, knowing that they are my greatest source of joy and fulfillment.

Navigating the world as a single parent has its challenges, but it has also taught me resilience and strength. Each obstacle I've faced has only made me more determined to create a better life for myself and my children, and I'm proud of how far we've come.

Though Matthew was my last relationship, I've made peace with the idea of remaining single for the time being. My focus is on raising my children and nurturing the bond we share, rather than seeking out romantic entanglements that may not be right for us.

Self-love and acceptance have become my guiding principles, allowing me to embrace my independence and live life on my own terms. I no longer feel the need to answer to anyone else or seek validation from external sources—I am enough, just as I am.

That being said, there are moments when loneliness creeps in, when I yearn for the companionship and support of a partner. But I've learned to cherish these moments of solitude, using them as opportunities for self-reflection and growth.

While I may entertain the idea of finding love again in the future, I refuse to settle for anything less than what I deserve—a partner who not only treats me well but also embraces my children as their own.

In the meantime, I focus on building a fulfilling life for myself and my children, surrounded by love, laughter, and the endless possibilities that the future holds. And though the road ahead may be uncertain, I face it with courage and optimism, knowing that whatever challenges may come our way, we will overcome them together, as a family.

So, as I look back on my journey thus far, I can't help but feel a sense of pride and gratitude for how far we've come. Life may not always be easy, but it's the challenges we face that shape us into the resilient, capable individuals we are meant to be.

And so, I embrace the present moment, cherishing the love and laughter that fills our home, and eagerly anticipating the adventures that lie ahead. For in the end, it's not the destination that matters, but the journey itself—and I'm grateful to be on this journey with my children by my side.